Walking the
Dartmoor Waterways

A Guide to retracing the leats and canals
of the Dartmoor country

Eric Hemery

DAVID & CHARLES
Newton Abbot   London   North Pomfret (Vt)

The author and publishers wish to emphasise that walkers should gain permission from the owner before entering any private property.

Mileage distances given at the start of each chapter relate to the length of the walk outlined in the following text, rather than to the length of the waterway.

Maps by Ethan Danielson

British Library Cataloguing in Publication Data
Hemery, Eric
  Walking the Dartmoor waterways : a guide to
  retracing the leats and canals of Dartmoor
  country.
  1. Inland navigation—England—Dartmoor (Devon)
  2. Dartmoor (England)—Description and travel—
  Guide-books
  I. Title
  914.23′5304858   DA670.D2

  ISBN 0-7153-8627-1

© Eric Hemery 1986

Photoset in Linotron Plantin by
Northern Phototypesetting Co, Bolton
and printed in Great Britain by
A. Wheaton & Co Ltd, Exeter
for David & Charles Publishers plc
Brunel House, Newton Abbot, Devon

Published in the United States of America
by David & Charles Inc
North Pomfret, Vermont 05053, USA

Contents

Foreword

In this country we are surrounded by water and surrounded by history. Dartmoor is fascinating in both respects.

It is hard to imagine sometimes that those simple channels of water – the leats – have played such an important part in the development of industry and growing prosperity of towns.

The Plymouth Leat, or Drake's Leat, which trapped the waters of the River Meavy (or Mewy), was an important, indeed vital, source of public water supply for Plymouth for 300 years, and the later Devonport Leat collecting the waters of the West Dart, Cowsic and Blacka Brook high up on Dartmoor, is still a valuable source for South West Water today.

To step into a disused part of the leats is to step into history; to walk both the leats and canals is to wonder at the ingenuity and enterprise of man.

Eric Hemery has provided a detailed and absorbing account to guide you pleasantly along the paths of the past.

Len Hill CBE JP
Chairman
South West Water

Introduction and Acknowledgements

If the multitudinous natural streams of Dartmoor were counted as 'waterways', there would be no end to this book. Even were all the mine and 'pot-water' leats included, they would number many hundreds. Selection has therefore been made to include the most historic leats and those situated in places of particular scenic interest. Canals pose no such problem: only two were built (and a third proposed) in the Dartmoor country, and another to carry Dartmoor ores to the river Tamar.

The practice of channelling water by gravity from intake to working-point is of great antiquity, still primitively in operation today in the Orient – especially in India and the Middle East. In ancient times, canals, both for irrigation and the passage of vessels, were built by the Assyrians, Egyptians and Babylonians, whose King Nebuchadnezzar built a 400 mile (644 km) canal from the Euphrates to the Persian Gulf. There is no sign on Dartmoor of the cutting of leats by the prehistoric hut dwellers, but evidence remains to show that it was undertaken in early medieval times – even perhaps by the Saxon settlers. The Romans were masters of canal, aqueduct and conduit construction, as seen so impressively at their hot-springs baths at Bath and in the celebrated aqueduct at Pont du Gard in France.

The Dartmoor pronunciation of 'leat' is 'late', just as that of 'cleave' is 'clave'. The word long ago became the name origin of Lade Hill in East Dart country, which is crossed by the Vitifer leat (see p102), the 't' of late (ie leat) becoming hardened to 'd' in the linked syllables.

Leats are numerous on the high moor, but there are no boat canals; those described in Part 3, traversing the border-country, were designed to transport merchandise between border-town or working-head and coast – or at least to a river link with the coast, such as a tidal estuary. In contrast to a canal, where water levels are controlled by lock gates, a leat operates exclusively by gravity flow, and a keen sense of the lie of the land was needed by the leat surveyor. Also, whereas

5

professional engineers are needed in designing and constructing a canal, the cutting of a leat may be described as a vernacular craft – even when the professional surveyor (such as John Taylor) entered upon the mine-leat scene in the late eighteenth century – as the work was usually entrusted to local tinners, who were experts in leat-cutting and tunnel-drivage. The Cornish word 'Wheal', a mine, is also a frequently found prefix to the names of Dartmoor mines; and it should be pointed out that moorland mine-leating systems are incomparably more complex than those of drinking-water and domestic leats, due to the spasms of closure and re-opening to which most of the mines were subject and the cutting of fresh channels to improve the water supply with each successive venture in order to drive larger and more powerful water-wheels.

The majority of moorland farms are sited near reliable springs; domestic water was usually leated from spring to farm court, where a dipping trough or well was provided for the farm-wife, the supply entering over a lip-stone. Water for general farm purposes was often a supplementary supply leated from the local stream and known on the Moor as a 'potwater' leat, or gutter; this normally entered the court and was sometimes deviated into subsidiary channels – dairy, calves' house, stable, shippen and so on. Much ingenuity was sometimes shown in carrying this out, with granite-lined conduits to contain the flow and tiny footbridges to facilitate crossing. Vinneylake (Mewy) provides one of the best examples of this canalising of the farm supply, although the desertion of the farm in *c*1925 (it is in the Burrator catchment area) now makes ready interpretation difficult.

Leats still in use, some now fulfilling a purpose different from the original, are more numerous than might commonly be supposed; they form Part 1 of this book, and disused leats, Part 2. Canals are described in Part 3. A flowing leat needs regular maintenance by cleaning and banking. Another relevant skill of the tinners was in cutting hillside drainage channels, by which means rainfall, which otherwise would escape haphazardly to the valley floor, was captured and channelled to a working-point. Small reservoirs were often built to retain water from such channels, examples existing on Shapley Common (Bovey) and at Yealm Falls (lower blowing house, left bank).

The traditional method of bridging a Dartmoor leat is by a single-opening clapper bridge, of which the great majority, relevant to this book, are recorded. Modern bridges of timber, concrete or girders are mentioned only if of practical use to the walker. An additional method of crossing a wide leat was provided by building into one bank a protruding stone from which a person might jump to the opposite bank; these are alluded to in the text as 'leap-stones'.

As may be judged from the channel distance given under each heading, leatside walks vary greatly in length. There is further the point that lengthy border-country reaches of leats are often not accessible to the public, though the author has been enabled to record and describe them here through the kind co-operation of landowners and tenants. Such no-access areas are clearly detailed in the text. The open reaches of the leats – which certainly exceed those of no-access – provide rewarding through-valley views and walking conditions which, if at times wet underfoot, do by their nature exclude strenuous hill-climbs. A separate introductory note relevant to canal-side walking appears at the beginning of Part 3. Map references are given where necessary to assist in locating the head and/or lower terminal of a leat. Direction of description, whether upstream or down and chosen according to the best scenic effect for the walker's enjoyment, is stated at the head of each 'Following the leat' section, and it will help the walker to remember that the terms 'right' and 'left' bank pertain always to the direction of flow. Dartmoor waterways and railroads sometimes lie in parallel, and the reader may find it helpful to consult chapters 1, 2 and 6 of the author's *Walking the Dartmoor Railroads*. Farm fields through which the walker is permitted to pass are numbered successively in the direction of the walk; in the case of two leats passing through the same series of fields where the direction of walk is UP for one and DOWN for the other, the number order is not changed and will therefore appear in reverse for one leat.

It is certainly the author's hope that the reader, setting out to view these labours of a past age – labours devoted to harnessing Dartmoor's pure waters to man's bodily and industrial needs – will derive not only enjoyment but a realisation of the local skills and tenacity exercised, often under trying conditions, on this great upland of wild, rocky slopes and rain-laden winds.

NOTE: place-names in the book at variance with Ordnance Survey versions are in accordance with those researched and given in the author's *High Dartmoor: Land and People*; they now appear on *Harvey's Mountain Map – Dartmoor*.

All six-figure map references given in the text relate to Square SX of the National Grid.

The author wishes to express his gratitude to the undermentioned persons for their kind co-operation, assistance and courtesy:

K. A. Ballamy of Newton Abbot; K. C. Baxter; E. Blatchford of DNPA; Mrs D. Cook of Plymouth; Ernie Bowden of Gidleigh; Mrs E. A. Buttigieg of Teigngrace; A. Cole of Dousland; T. W. Eggins of Dousland; Norman Fry of Lydford; John W. German of Roborough; Reverend P. G. Harrison, Vicar of Holne; John Hearn of Whitchurch; Mrs Mary Hood, Maristow Estate Manager; Miss V. James of Mary Tavy; Will Jordan of Moortown; Sydney King of Newton Abbot; Tony Lewis of Ashburton; Ross Mitchell of SWW; Major J. D. Parkinson of Yelverton; Sam Payne of Newton Abbot; Fred Pote of Merivale; David Powell of Holne; J. F. Roberts of Watts, Blake & Bearne; John Robins of Tavistock; F. D. Robinson of Horrabridge; L. Rogers of Horrabridge; Alec Shaw of Meavy; Harold Skelly of Dousland; Brian Skilton of Horrabridge; Mrs A. Skinner and staff of the Local History Department of Plymouth City Library; B. A. Stanswood of Mary Tavy; A. G. Stephens of Horndon; W. Vanstone of Meavy; Sid Warren of Peter Tavy; A. Whieldon of Horrabridge; Dr R. C. Young of Dousland.

Documentary information given in Walk 12 is derived from the Morley Estate Papers in The West Devon Record Office, Plymouth.

1
Devonport Leat

21¼ miles (34.2km)   Map 1

Historical digest
This remarkable waterway amply demonstrates the skills possessed by eighteenth-century water engineers. Fed by three adjacent, parallel moorland river systems, it carried over 2 million gallons (4.5 million litres) of fresh water daily to Devonport town and dockyard. The yard used always to be known as Plymouth Dock, or simply Dock, and the water supply consequently as 'Dock Leat'.

The need for a copious supply for Devonport is apparent from Dr Samuel Johnson's comments on the occasion of his visit to Plymouth with Sir Joshua Reynolds in 1762. As K. C. Baxter wrote in the *Western Morning News* on 13th December 1984 (the second centenary of Johnson's death):

> At the time of Johnson's visit to Devon the expansion of the dockyard encouraged the growth of a new town, now Devonport, and, as a consequence, a rivalry between it and Plymouth. It pleased Johnson to ally himself with the old against the new; and he lost no occasion of inveighing against the rogue 'dockers' as he called them. Such aliens and upstarts must not be allowed to share Plymouth's water supply.
> 'Let them die of thirst. They shall not have a drop.' This was said with all his usual vigour of utterance, but was, of course, completely at variance with his profound and habitual compassion for poor fallen mankind.

The leat, when it eventually arrived to succour the 'rogue dockers' was, like all open channels, subject to pollution and blockage by winter ice and snow-drifts. The Burrator undertaking of 1898 to supply the entire Plymouth-Devonport area ended a century of growing difficulties for 'Dock' in particular, which had steadily grown during the eighty or so years since the construction of the leat, and where hundreds of men had been drafted in to build naval vessels to serve in the war against Napoleon. Frank Howarth wrote in *The Plymouth Water Undertaking* (1934):

Powers to take water from the West Dart, Cowsic and Blackabrook were obtained in 1793 by the Company of Proprietors of the Plymouth Dock Waterworks. Under these powers the company erected weirs on the three streams and diverted the water into leats, all three leats meeting at a point north of the Princetown Convict Prison. From this point the leat contoured the hill via Tor Royal, Peat Cot and Whiteworks, then passed into the Meavy watershed through a tunnel about 640 yards in length, crossed the River Meavy in an iron shute or launder and then contoured the opposite hill via Dousland, Yelverton, Roborough and Crownhill to Devonport. The leat had not to exceed 10 feet in breadth and it is still in use as far as Dousland, a length of 17 miles. From there the water is conveyed in pipes.

Under the Act the company were authorised to supply water within the towns of Plymouth Dock, Stoke Damarel, Stonehouse and the parts adjacent. The Company of Proprietors of the Plymouth Dock Waterworks afterwards became the Devonport Water Company and their undertaking was purchased in 1902 by the then Devonport Corporation.

The upper system of conflowing leats is still in use as far as Burrator, for which reason its overall course is included here in Part 1 with 'flowing leats'. It is essentially a leat to follow upstream, for the transition from lowlands to border-country and high moorland, in that order, is quite dramatic. As in the case of the Plymouth leat, it is not possible to follow the in-country reach, but only to inspect short, remaining sections of it: it passes northward from city to farmland and private estate to emerge on Roborough Down, where description will begin. The leat's course within the city area is in any case now almost untraceable due to building development. A short section, now preserved by the dead rather than the living, lies in the old burial ground of St Pancras's Church, Pennycross, where it passes between the graves as a shallow, green trench – a desolate oasis amidst vast areas of modern development that have completely swallowed it. Vandalised and neglected, the graveyard is forlorn to a degree. To see the relic, drive along Pennycross Road to St Pancras' Church Hall; the entrance to the graveyard is on the opposite (east) roadside. The impressive buildings of the Royal Engineering College at Manadon are seen from the old channel, pinpointing an upstream stage on the leat, which reached Pennycross by serpentine contour-looping.

10

North of Manadon the leat follows the moat of the old Crownhill Fort and enters the grounds of the SWW treatment works; it has a tunnel junction with the Plymouth leat (see p77), passes behind the Castle Service Station and alongside the east boundary of the waterworks' grounds, where it is bridged for the entrance drive and runs, again underground, to Looseleigh Lane en route for Roborough.

A brief account of visible portions of the leat in the Maristow estate grounds may be of interest to the reader. The author was enabled to inspect these by courtesy of the estate manager, although **they are not accessible to the public.** In the grounds beyond Higher Lodge the leat emerges from Common Lane Plantation and crosses an open space in the park, giving a fine view of Maristow House, to a granite arch-bridge carrying an estate road. From the bridge the leat runs through a copse to a bridge beneath another road descending to Henshears Farm. A short way beyond the road it makes an abrupt bend to descend a hillside field where, funnelled by the Henshears valley, there are magnificent views of the foot of Tavy spanned by the estuary railway bridge, the River Tamar, Bere Ferrers, Saltash and Tamerton Foliot. The leat now passes beneath another arch-bridge on the old Henshears Farm track from Roborough Common, and through the next field to reach the south-westernmost corner of the common; here it enters upon open ground – where it can be seen by the walker – before passing into two more fields, which it contours to reach Roborough Plantation, where the channel is much overgrown.

The original terminal of the leat was a small reservoir in Devonport Park, Moricetown, from which the overflow was conducted to the River Tamar nearby. About 1825, Rowden's reservoir was built with a capacity of 2,071,000 gallons (9.5m litres), to which the leat was then diverted to supply dockyard and town. The channel passed Swilly Cottage, near Ham Lodge, and ran northward above Pennycross to Manadon, Powesland and Crownhill reservoir (1875); from thence it led to Belliver reservoir (1898), crossed the Tamerton road and reached the Maristow estate near Roborough House, passing through woodlands and across the fields of Henshears Farm into Common Lane Plantation. Car-parking space is plentiful in the Roborough Down-Clearbrook area and need not be

11

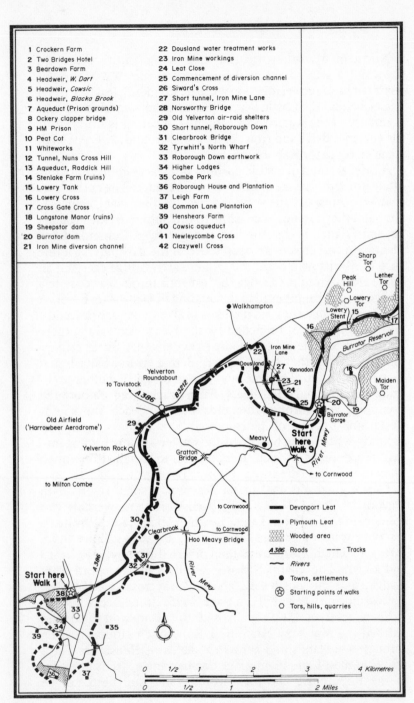

1 Crockern Farm
2 Two Bridges Hotel
3 Beardown Farm
4 Headweir, *W. Dart*
5 Headweir, *Cowsic*
6 Headweir, *Blacka Brook*
7 Aqueduct (Prison grounds)
8 Ockery clapper bridge
9 HM Prison
10 Peat Cot
11 Whiteworks
12 Tunnel, Nuns Cross Hill
13 Aqueduct, Raddick Hill
14 Stenlake Farm (ruins)
15 Lowery Tank
16 Lowery Cross
17 Cross Gate Cross
18 Longstone Manor (ruins)
19 Sheepstor dam
20 Burrator dam
21 Iron Mine diversion channel

22 Dousland water treatment works
23 Iron Mine workings
24 Leat Close
25 Commencement of diversion channel
26 Siward's Cross
27 Short tunnel, Iron Mine Lane
28 Norsworthy Bridge
29 Old Yelverton air-raid shelters
30 Short tunnel, Roborough Down
31 Clearbrook Bridge
32 Tyrwhitt's North Wharf
33 Roborough Down earthwork
34 Higher Lodges
35 Combe Park
36 Roborough House and Plantation
37 Leigh Farm
38 Common Lane Plantation
39 Henshears Farm
40 Cowsic aqueduct
41 Newleycombe Cross
42 Clazywell Cross

Map 1 showing Walk 1 Devonport Leat and Walk 9 Plymouth (or Drake's) Leat

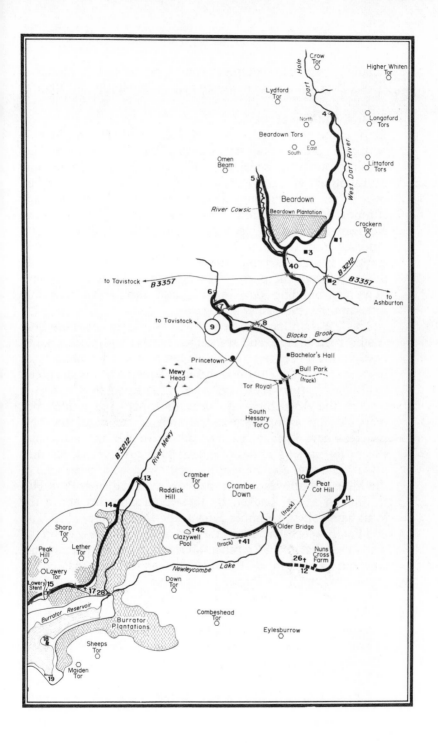

detailed here. The complete course of the leat is shown as 'Dock Leat' on the OS one-inch map (first edition) of 1809.

Following the leat (UP)

Start at the southwest corner of Roborough Down (503637) where a portion of the channel can be seen passing (downstream) from one field (right) below a wall-bridging stone into another (left), from where it has been infilled and ploughed over as far as Roborough Plantation. Next, follow the track running northward beside the east boundary wall of the Maristow grounds to reach the point (504644) where the leat emerges from Common Lane Plantation and passes below a clapper bridge carrying the track. The channel is easily followed from here to Yelverton and Dousland where, however, building development and farmlands inevitably interrupt the leat-walker's progress.

The leat is unlined for a short way as it approaches the Bere Alston road-bridge, and walking is easy along the left bank; beyond this it becomes overgrown but rewards the walker with his first view of the Dartmoor heights. Crossed by a wide, green road – the pre-turnpike Chagford-Plymouth packhorse track – it reaches the A386 highway, beneath which it is infilled but reappears on a gorse-infested stretch of common; the best progress here is achieved by walking in the leat bed, clear except for minor patches of gorse. As it curves (left) to enter upon Yelverton golf course, the first clear, wide panorama of the Moor's southwest escarpment opens ahead from Peak Hill to Shaugh Moor, backed by the western heights above the Walkham valley, Cramber Down, the Plym ridge, Shiel Top and Pen Beacon. The line of the leat can actually be seen on the distant south flank of Cramber (above the Burrator plantations) where its elevation is 700ft (213m) greater than that of the present viewpoint. Clapper bridges carry tracks crossing the down, and wooden bridges exist for the convenience of golfers as the leat progresses; for although already disused when the golf course was laid down, the depth and width of the channel – in which water lies after heavy rainfall – could present awkward obstacles to the golfers. It is pleasant to turn aside for a moment to survey the splendid view described.

The old building with the undulating roof seen below, right, is Tyrwhitt's Clearbrook North Wharf depot on his 1823 Plymouth & Dartmoor Railway. The Clearbrook road passes beyond the building and the leat is now joined in parallel by the lines of the P&DR and Plymouth leat. Passing beneath a succession of three granite clapper bridges – one of six imposts now collapsing – the leat approaches the fields of Chubb Tor (Clearbrook); both Plymouth leat and P&DR enter the fields, but the Devonport leat swings left outside the hedges and enters a tunnel 215yd (197m) long beneath a small ridge. The end-portals of border-slate stand 3ft 9in (1.1m) above the leat bed; an old track ascends from Clearbrook beside the Chubb Tor hedges and crosses the tunnel near the southeast portal. The purpose of the tunnel was to avoid an inconvenient proximity between the two historic leats, especially having regard to a marginal note on the original copy of the Act of 1793, which ruled that 'the Plymouth Leat [was] not to be affected'. This ruling certainly would have been infringed had the Devonport leat also contoured the ridge within the fields instead of flowing underground.

Both leats and tramroad now continue in proximity to the Chubbtor road; this was actually formed on the tramroad and many granite sets are seen *in situ*. Houses bordering the road are of mid- to late-twentieth century origin, but slip roads leading from the A386 highway to the Chubbtor road are nevertheless bridged across the Devonport channel, here a wide, deep ditch. Nearer Yelverton the leat passes beneath both tramroad and highway, to which it makes an oblique approach; the channel disappears into a reinforced concrete duct beneath the road and receives drainage from the World War II Harrowbeer airfield – still known as Yelverton aerodrome – through a supplementary duct, each typical of wartime construction. A transverse, wooden fence runs from the roadside to a wall bounding the private houses, right, and a wicket gate is seen in the fence near the wall (beyond which is the Plymouth leat channel).

To see the Devonport channel on the west side of the highway (if motoring north) turn into the Buckland road just before reaching Yelverton roundabout; immediately turn left onto the airfield road passing the old air-raid shelters; park at shelter 1. Walk to the rear of shelter 2; observe the fence below the further roadside and, just beyond it, the hollow of the channel emerging from the concrete duct. No duct is visible here on the west side, but manhole covers give access to the buried airfield drainage pipe below shelters 2 and 3. Turn about and follow the mostly blocked channel past shelter 2 to shelter 1, where it approaches the highway in a clear curve behind the second bay of the shelter, exactly aligned with the Yelverton shops. The rather complicated lines-of-communication pattern at Yelverton is as follows: the P&DR crosses the Green; the infilled Devonport leat lies below the road fronting the shops, whilst the Plymouth leat passes at the rear of the buildings. The Devonport channel reappears beyond the shops as a shallow ditch in a private garden in Morella Road, passes beneath the bridge in Westella Road and enters Lake Farm field 1.

Next drive from Westella Road to Cowards Lake Farm caravan, Lake Lane, show a copy of this book and ask permission of Mr or Mrs A. Cole to follow the leat through fields 4–1 to the bridge in Lake Lane; this they have kindly agreed to extend to personal callers. This step is very worthwhile as both the leats and the old GWR Princetown branch pass through Mr Cole's fields. Return to Westella Road and enter field 4, where the channel is infilled; move to the right, therefore, and follow the Plymouth channel from its bridge to a gateway on the further side of the field. Enter field 3 via the Plymouth leat; the Devonport channel is now visible, left, and the two leats cross fields 3 and 2 in very close proximity for a short way, the GWR meanwhile bearing away to the left. Twin clapper bridges (Pl.10) appear in field 2 beneath, unusually, cedar trees, and the Devonport channel passes into the garden of Leat Cottage, Lake Lane. Continue beside the Plymouth channel into and across field 1; pass through the gateway ahead into Lake Lane beside the Plymouth leat bridge.

Rejoin the Devonport leat by walking westward along Lake Lane to its point of emergence from Leat Cottage, where it crosses beneath the lane. It is then clearly seen crossing a field (right) bordered by the B3212 highway, so that entry into the field is unnecessary. Also seen, for good measure, are the Plymouth leat (right), the raised trackbed of the P&DR (left) and the GWR embankment curving towards a large bus garage beside the highway. The Devonport leat was crossed by the GWR before reaching Leat Cottage and now makes a direct approach to the highway, where the bridge parapets remain to mark the leat's passage beneath it into a field opposite: here it swings right to run along the north roadside hedge. Its approach to Dousland may be seen from the bridge at the entrance road to 'Rockleaze' (there is a prominent name-board, and the channel is carrying water, an overflow from Dousland reservoir which enters a grating near Rockleaze). Next comes a brief channel diversion at Merrivale Terrace and the leat passes before Dousland House, beneath the Walkhampton branch road (opposite the Burrator Inn) and again below the highway, where it is bridged on the east verge at the entrances to private houses. The channel continues parallel with the highway, but now within the grounds of Dousland treatment works, where alum and lime are added to the impounded water from the Burrator pipeline (see p19). It makes an abrupt bend over a stepped bed to approach an enormous sluice of wood and ironwork, which once controlled the supply of water into the old Dousland reservoir. From here the actual bed of the channel is expertly paved for a short way and well preserved in its passage across five farm fields; **these must not be entered,** but the leat can be viewed clearly from the near distance, so proceed as follows: *field 1* (where sluice is situated beside boundary wall of treatment works), look over an iron gate beside the highway at 539692; both sluice and channel crossing the field to the further side are visible; beyond this it can be viewed from the south side of Yannadon Down. Take the Meavy road from Dousland crossroads and turn left at the first cross-lanes; this is Iron Mine Lane. After crossing a cattle-grid, notice the leat bridge parapets; continue round the (left) bend at the top of the lane and park on open ground beyond the houses; walk westward along the track (this is the P&DR: observe granite sets); look down on fields 1–5 and the water treatment works. Field 1 is identifiable by the 'itching' post in the centre and the clapper bridge near the hedge. *Field 2*: a clapper bridge stands near the west hedge and Walkhampton Church (right) appears to be at the same level as the field. Near the hedge the right bank has been lowered to form an entry for water from a diversion channel; this was made in the early years of the nineteenth century, when surface work began on the south flank of Yannadon to raise iron ore, to bypass the mine. This diversion channel is infilled to within a short distance from the east hedge, where its sunken bed is clearly seen passing through a breach in the hedge. *Field 3*: a small clapper bridge appears on the main channel. The diversion channel crosses the northwest corner of the field into a short tunnel passing obliquely beneath the track (P&DR) and having a low, arched portal at each end. *Field 4*: a massive clapper cart-bridge of five imposts stands beside the east hedge. *Field 5*: the channel disappears into a private garden before passing beneath Iron Mine Lane.

Two features in these fields specifically illustrate the expert workmanship employed in the construction of the leat's main channel – the evenness of the granite-slab lining, and the care expended on rounding the opposing ends of hedges breached to admit the leat. East of Iron Mine Lane the leat is in a ruinous state as it passes through more private gardens, and its crossing of Leat Close is no longer in evidence. Entering the garden of 'Caritas' it runs near the house and emerges onto the open moor of Yannadon at 542682, where it passes beneath a clapper bridge carrying a track beside the outer enclosure wall and offers a splendid view over the lower Mewy valley to Gutter Tor, Ringmoor Down, Saddlesborough and Wigford Down; the rural delight of all this is much enhanced, during school playtime, by the sound rising from the valley of playing children in the grounds of Meavy Primary School. On rounding the down the view widens to include Shiel Top, the Plym ridge and Eylesburrow; central to the moorscape are Sheepstor village and Sheeps Tor, Down Tor, Cramber (where, again, the distant course of the leat is visible), the three fine tors of Lowery, Lether and Sharp, and the blunt cap of Peak Hill.

The diversion channel, emerging from the tunnel, is deeply sunken in ascending the unenclosed south flank of Yannadon where, of course, it may freely be followed. Unlined and apparently hastily cut, it does not show the signs of expertise expended on the main channel; it would have been incumbent upon the mine owners to cut the diversion channel and they doubtless used their own workers for the task. The walker can follow either the main or diversion channel, though the latter, despite being in places choked by furze, is the more interesting, being traceable from its tunnel beneath the P&DR to the junction with the main channel high on the slope of Yannadon, about ½ mile (.8km) from the mine workings. The junction occurs beside a 'PCWW 1917' stone (see p80) erected on the leat's left bank. A difference in level between the two channels – the diversion being slightly the higher – prompts the question, how could the water enter it? The answer is, I believe, that no such problem existed when the diversion channel was cut, perhaps only twenty years after the building of the main leat. If the apparently unsuccessful, short-lived operations at the iron mine terminated – as the lack of records suggests – before the half-century, steps would then have been taken to block the diversion intake and restrict the water to the main channel, which then carried its load at some velocity along the flank of Yannadon for a further half-century. This would account for the deeply eroded bed of the main channel at this point, where the water has cut down from 1 to 2ft (.3 to .6m). It is interesting to note that seven parallel lines score the side of Yannadon above the Mewy Valley here: from highest to lowest they are a stony (but grass-grown) track from Dousland to Burrator Halt, the Iron Mine diversion channel, the main Devonport channel, a tinners' hillside drainage channel, the old GWR Princetown trackbed, the Burrator-Dousland road and the Plymouth leat.

The curvature of the down soon brings into sight the waters of Burrator reservoir; during my fieldwork for this chapter in 1985 the lake was completely frozen over and dusted with a light coating of snow. A short way below the leat are the kissing gates on either side of the GWR track at Burrator Halt, and a view of startling beauty. The leat, soon to be crossed by the GWR, is from here rather overgrown, a condition which improves when the walker reaches the live flow of the leat. At a point above the grounds of the Lodge (the water superintendent's house) 2.9 million gallons (13m litres) of water daily pass through a grating into a rotary screening device and a pipeline conveying it to Dousland treatment works and reservoir, from where it is piped to numerous supply points. The spectacular waterfall above the lakeside road – captured by the cameras of so many visitors in the belief that it is a part of the natural scene – is merely water diverted from the pipeline into the reservoir as surplus to requirements. This overflow once worked an electricity generator at the Lodge, but the waterworks there were connected to the mains supply in September 1981.

Follow the path beside the flowing leat through the plantations; it diverges from the railway (just above it) and reaches Woodland Hill near the piers of the dismantled railway bridge. Cross the lane and continue along the leatside path, when a bend in the channel brings a good view up the Mewy valley. The leat passes below the Lowery road; mount the bank and stile, left, and follow the path through the plantations a little above the leat. Passing a rock bearing six slots from a granite mason's 'jumper', the path reaches a gateway and stone stile; mount the stile, cross a broad, green track descending from a quarry under Lowery Tor (left); the track, Lowery Stent, crosses the leat clapper and reaches a road junction at Lower Lowery, where once stood a granite cross – for the lane here is the ancient Buckfast/Buckland/Tavistock monastic way.

Ahead, the leat is seen to pass between the walls of an open granite chamber known as Lowery Tank, its masonry expertly constructed and once a means of measuring the flow of the leat. The old fields here are those of Higher and Lower Lowery Farms; the leat passes below a wide clapper carrying the road and flows along the latter's further (east) verge. Alongside a flood-relief sluice is another wide cart clapper, now provided with parapets, giving access to Lowery Moor and Vinneylake Farm. (It may be understood that the farms in the Mewy watershed mentioned in this chapter are all now in ruins, the occupants having been obliged by the Plymouth water authority to abandon them during the 1920s.)

Beyond Lowery Bridge the tarmac road recrosses the leat and descends steeply to Norsworthy Bridge. The line of the monastic way is continued, however, by the rough track to Riddipit Steps and Lether Tor Bridge. On the left bank of the leat stands Cross Gate Cross; the now vanished gate controlled entry to Vinneylake and Norsworthy Farms. At the point where the track starts to descend (also steeply) to the river, the leat enters the next plantation-stand below the massive clitter and mighty steeple of Lether Tor and crags of nearby Lowery Tor. Beyond a stile is a noisy cataract; a clapper spans the leat at the head of the rise and two slotted posts are seen, beyond which the channel levels out into a soundless glide, enabling one to hear the boisterous progress of the river below.

Crumbling, moss-covered walls with ancient gateways creep from Lether Tor Farm towards the leat, which shoots a clapper cart-bridge carrying an old track from the farm to the Walkham valley. Flood-control sluices occur, one with fine slotted stones, beyond which the plantations end as the open moor rises beyond Stenlake Farm. Mount the stile and notice the walled lane descending (from the highway above) to the farm, where the Gill family were occupants at the turn of the century. Octogenerian Mrs D. Cook of Plymouth, neé Gill, tells me that in hot summer weather she and her brother used to enjoy splashing in the cool waters of the leat – an activity positively discouraged by the present water authority!

The walker now enters upon a beautiful, unspoilt reach of the Mewy valley enhanced by the ruggedness of the open moor. Traffic moves between Yelverton and Princetown along the B3212 road on the flank of Leedon Hill (above, left); Black Tor rises ahead and Hart Tor, right. Beyond the farm the leat is aqueducted over the valley of Stean Lake by a curved, finely built, high-banked channel; follow the right bank upstream; pass a wide cart clapper, a hut circle, a footbridge, a flood-relief sluice and some drilled, slotted stones including some old tramroad sets which presumably were brought from the P&DR after the line became disused over a century ago, to be used in banking the leat (*cf* p72). Soon comes a view of the rocky dell of Blacktor Hole and, above and beyond it, the partly afforested site of Princetown railway station and the stationmaster's house. Black Tor appears, left, with its prominently poised (but now immovable) logan stone, and, below it, the bend in the leat at Iron Bridge.

This well known beauty spot is scarcely enhanced by the iron pipe delivering the waters of Hartor Brook into the leat, but compensation exists in the sparkling cascade on the west slope of Raddick Hill. The cover picture shows the water crossing the aqueduct and a stepped bed into the continuing channel; the aqueduct, 'Iron Bridge', is supported still by the original granite piers of the 1792 timber aqueduct. Cross it along the north side and ascend the steep, rocky path to the high plain of Raddick Hill. The old transverse channel on the hillside is that of the Keaglesborough leat which, as Keaglesborough Mine was working when the Devonport was cut, had to be

21

aqueducted across it. Pass a flood-relief sluice near the hilltop
and notice the Bronze Age hut village near the left bank. The
scene viewed from the plain is very fine. The leat channel here is
mentioned on page 14 as being visible from Roborough Down;
from right to left are Cramber Tor (near distance); the large
dome of Eylesburrow (mid-distance); the Plym ridge and
Trowlesworthy Tors; Gutter Tor on the east tip of Ringmoor
Down; Sheeps Tor; Wigford Down; the in-country reaching to
Plymouth Sound; a glimpse of Burrator Lake; Lowery and
Lether Tors, Peak Hill and Sharp Tor; Leedon Hill and Tor;
Cocks Tor, Mid Steeple Tor and Roos Tor (distant), and
Foggin Tor (mid-distance).

Interesting features occur upstream. Beyond Clazywell
Bridge (a cart clapper), the leat contour-loops a pleasant little
re-entrant at the southwest foot of Cramber; from here, in
addition to the view described above, are seen Black Tor (now
insignificantly low), Brent Tor, Swell and Great Steeple Tors
and Great Mis Tor. A dismantled sluice here once diverted
flood water into Dead Lake.

Beyond the re-entrant the leat is banked above the head of a
deep tinners' gert to a height of 18ft (5.5m). It crosses a second
gert in similar fashion and brings into view a row of tinners'
mounds on a distant hill ahead; these denote Nuns Cross Hill,
where the line of the leat can be seen rounding the hill-slope
past a waterman's hut. From here also is seen, right, the outline
of Clazywell Cross on the Buckfast monastic way. Sabine
Baring-Gould, in his book on Sheepstor, states that in 1844
when the leat was very low – he mistakenly names it as the
Plymouth leat – water was pumped from the pool 'in large
quantities to fill the leat. Its [the pool's] depth was then
ascertained'. Baring-Gould gives no figure, but his
contemporary, Robert Burnard, found the depth of the pool to
be not more than 20ft (6.1m).

Small footbridges span the leat, and banking around the gerts
is a sign that the latter had been worked out before 1792. Iron
valves have been inserted in the channel to control overflow into
the gerts; one has been removed and lies grassed-over on the
moor – an item almost of archaeological interest!

When Newleycombe Cross appears, the monastic way can be
seen converging with the leat in Older Bottom. More

footbridges occur, then the leat bends sharply (in Older Bottom) and the headwaters of Newleycombe Lake form a pleasant pool in a small gert, from which water cascades into the channel. The granite post seen from here on the north skyline is one of the series marking the boundary of the Forest of Dartmoor, which the walker will shortly enter. Notice a ford on each of the twin streams below, right, where the monastic way crosses the Newleycombe headwaters; its continuation is seen mounting to the skyline, right, beside the largest of the tinners' mounds already mentioned, on Nuns Cross Hill.

A skilfully engineered bend carries the leat across Older Bottom; another stream from Newleycombe Head enters the channel, below which a mire delivers water in fortuitous compensation to the stream at the fords. The course of the channel is now due south on the flank of Nuns Cross Hill; shooting a clapper bridge carrying the monastic way – for this portion of the old track has continued in use – it affords striking views over the tinners' pits, gerts and leats in Newleycombe Bottom (right). Bridges, sluices and weirs occur as the leat begins a corrective easterly curve round the spur of the hill to enter Drivage Bottom. Above the right bank stands a modern granite cross erected in 1968 by Lieutenant Commander B. Hutchinson of Stoke Fleming, in memory of his mother: the panelled inscriptions read SLH (west face) and $\frac{1887}{1966}$ (east face). At the head of this wild and lonely valley is the mouth of a tunnel (Pl. 1), driven to maintain the gravity flow of the leat for almost 700yd (640m) beneath the Dart-Mewy watershed. Tinners were employed for the tunelling, which was spoken of always as a 'drivage' – hence the name of the valley. The tunnel is a fine piece of water engineering, though it dates from some sixty years after the original leat was cut. The first tunnelling scheme utilised the linking together of several existing adits of Nuns Cross Mine and necessitated a slightly higher cut on the east flank of the hill; the resulting sluggish flow of the water was remedied only by this specially driven tunnel (c1850) and a new, lower-sited leat channel. Stand above the tunnel portal and notice the deepset, gleaming channel pointing to the southwestern tors against a background of the Cornish moorland.

Look out for a ruined building on the north side of the little

Plate 1   Devonport Leat Tunnel – Drivage Bottom: Notice the expert masonry of c1850. The leat is flowing towards the camera point

valley near the tunnel. Known to the farmers of Nuns Cross as 'Old Farm', this was adopted by the leat cutters to house a forge for making, repairing and sharpening their tools. Follow the line of the underground leat by maintaining its easterly direction; the splendid Siward's Cross ('Nuns Cross' is a modern name) rises to the left and the early twentieth-century building of Nuns Cross Farm – a farm no longer – stands gauntly alongside the heaped ruins of the original, single-storey

24

farmhouse of 1871. The enclosure wall fronting the buildings forms a guide to the upstream tunnel mouth; here, an iron tunnel-gate and a SWW signboard are seen, a short length of leat is fenced in, and a feeder from Nuns Cross Mire (right) entering the leat is bridged by a small clapper.

The walker will from now on remain in Dart country, from whence the peat-laden waters of the upper Devonport leat are drawn. The scenic contrast to the view from the west tunnel portal is, as so often when crossing a Dartmoor watershed, dramatically striking. Lonely desolation stretches ahead beneath the bold slopes of Eylesburrow Common to Hand Hill, Stream Hill, Crane Hill and Caters Beam. The well-marked Nuns Cross Ford serves an old peat and mining track, in heavy use a century and more ago, and a leat clapper carries the track beside a flood-relief sluice. On the hillside above the leat is the original cut leading to the first 'composite' tunnel mentioned above, an interesting historical feature; the absence of any lining of granite slabs is doubtless due to their removal for use in the new, lower channel now in use.

Eastward from here on a clear day are visible Goldsmith's Cross and Mount Misery Cross on the monastic way, this having ascended from Older Bottom (see above) to Siward's Cross, passed through the old Nuns Cross newtake and descended to a ford on Nuns Cross Brook, below right, from where it passes Goldsmith's Cross en route for Childe's Tomb (invisible from here). The walker will soon see two leats below (right) leading to the once busy Whiteworks tin mine (visible ahead); Goldsmith's Cross now appears under the lower of two scattered rockpiles just beyond the valley of Whealam Stream.

A short way further on, when Peat Cot Hill comes in view to the left of Whiteworks, the eastward panorama is at its best: the huge, wet spread of the notorious Foxtor Mire lies immediately below bordered, right, by the southern hill-chain and Fox Tor; beyond it, the east side of the central basin is backed by the Moor's eastern highlands. Watch for the stones of a kistvaen and retaining circle below the leat, from where Hey Tor is visible. At a breached wall ahead – known to the old moormen as Sunny Corner – the leat begins a northwesterly curve to approach the flank of Peat Cot Hill. Visible also is Castle Road (from Princetown) descending to Whiteworks, and beside a disused roadside quarry (a useful car-parking space favoured by walkers visiting this area), it crosses the converging leat on a sturdy clapper bridge with parapets.

Upstream from the quarry are seen, from right to left beyond the Swincombe valley, the tors of Rippen, Corndon, the tip of Bel Tor, Chinkwell and Honeybag Tors and the long, elevated ridge of Hameldon, whilst the cone of Bellever Tor rises in the mid-distance. The area threaded by the leat now becomes a convulsion of pits, mounds and infilled shafts worked a century ago in the heyday of Whiteworks Tin Mine. The leat executes two hairpin bends to contour re-entrants, one containing a clapper bridge. The site of the mine wheel-pits and dressing floors are near Stamps Gate and the north edge of Foxtor Mire. The lower of the ruined cottages at the terminus of the road was the birthplace of a notable man of Dartmoor named Jack Worth. With a memory reaching back to the days of the working mine, Jack had for many years assisted the hunt by regularly cleaning out the vital Black Lane peat pass; he died in Princetown in 1982.

As the walker rounds the spur of Peat Cot Hill he will see a clapper bridge (nineteenth-century, tare-and-feather cut) of five massive imposts spanning the leat, and the shallow, wet Strane valley opening below. The valley is overlooked by the cairn of Brockenborough on the opposite hill, the slope below it striped by the turf-ties worked by the old peat merchants of Peat Cot, and by the Whiteworks miners needing peat charcoal for the mine furnaces. The West Dart and Cowsic Tors appear in the north as the leat curves towards Peat Cot, and the Sherberton track at Strane Ford appears close by, below. As I walked the leat path on a cold November day, a *pair* of herons rose from Straneside, one with a squirming fish in its bill; below, two more leat channels once carried Strane water to the waterwheels of Whiteworks.

The hills and tors overlooking the headwaters of the Devonport leat are now in view: the Beardown Tors and Longaford Tor, Omen Beam (marked by Long Plantation) and Black Dunghill beyond. Near ahead are South Hessary Tor and the Tor Royal plantations. The leat banks in this reach, at the time of writing, are being reinforced and several piles of cut blocks lie ready alongside. The house first in view at the small, nineteenth-century settlement of Peat Cot is Peat Cot Farm, white-painted and with unexpected Gothic windows. Next is the chapel where several generations of the Worth family worshipped; Dartmoor's noted historian Richard Hansford Worth (1868–1950) was of this family, he and his wife often attending the chapel service on summer Sundays, when Mrs Worth would play the harmonium. Peat Cot Cottage lies beyond the chapel, and Castle Farm on the edge of the combe above. With the death of Miss Mabel Worth of Castle Farm in 1984, the last member of the resident Peat Cot clan left a scene where they had held sway for at least 200 years since the redoubtable Charlotte (and husband James) Worth founded the settlement soon after the Devonport leat was constructed.

On entering the hamlet, notice the nicely arched stone of the leatside stile. A track (left) running up to the open moor on Peat Cot Hill passes a triangular enclosure which was built as a pound. The leat describes a hairpin bend in the deep little combe, where a neat clapper footbridge links the two farms. Beyond the combe the leat has an uneventful course to Tor Royal. More stones for re-banking lie beside the channel, and at a point near the Tor Royal plantations an embanked level approaches the west side of the leat; its purpose is not at all clear, but it could have been built for a short tramroad to transport granite slabs from a small quarry (seen nearby) needed in the leat's construction. A track descends, left, from Castle Road to a wooden bridge over the leat. Below the left bank are old gateposts – certainly pre-dating the leat – and the wide desolation of Strane Head beyond. Visible now through the trees is the mansion known as Tor Royal, built for himself in 1785 by Sir Thomas Tyrwhitt, the remarkable man who built also the Plymouth & Dartmoor Railway and the Napoleonic War prison at Princetown. Two rabbit-buries in the enclosure beyond the right bank suggest that Sir Thomas and his guests were not averse to some sport to replenish the larder.

A (private) wooden clam leads through a copse into the Tor Royal grounds, the leat here flowing past an old farm building capped by a modern roof. Ahead is the bridge carrying the Tor Royal-Swincombe track – historically the Tavistock-Ashburton packhorse track, which received regular, heavy use before the construction of the 1792 turnpike road via Two Bridges. The

27

pleasant, grassy leatside path continues northward from the bridge above Bull Park Farm, where Bachelor's Hall Brook flows to join Blacka Brook.

Notice the old mine workings (left) of Bachelor's Hall Mine and, right, the long, low building of Bachelor's Hall Farm. This was once a mill and bakery supplying the war prison with bread, and the hillside now crossed by the leat is consequently known as Bakery Hill. Near ahead comes the first sighting of the prison complex at Princetown; the beautiful, tumbling stream under the hillside, right, is Blacka Brook, the prison being situated above the brook's right bank upstream and directly below North Hessary Tor. (The current of the leat in this reach is noticeably slow and deep.) Also ahead is the site of the strange old house known as the 'Ockery' – demolished following a tragedy within its walls during the early years of World War I – where captured Napoleonic officers had been permitted to live on parole until their repatriation from 1815 onwards. The very fine clapper bridge of two openings here once carried the Chagford-Plymouth packhorse track, another historic route of pre-turnpike times. The disused leat seen on the opposite hillside (right) formerly served Roundhill Farm, so named from the ball-like protuberance of Round Hill above it.

Between Bachelor's Hall and the Ockery are several interesting features: the prison, village and St Michael's Church ahead; a cart clapper bridge carrying a track to Bachelor's Hall; a fine specimen of a cornditch wall necessarily breached for the leat; several leap-stones; a flood-relief sluice and a small clapper carrying the path over the sluice; several well-engineered bends, carefully lined; substantial reinforce-ment of the left bank on the steep hillside above Blacka Brook; a good view of the upper West Dart valley under the tors of Crockern, Littaford, Longaford and Higher Whiten and, to the left of them, the Beardown Tors. To arrive here, the walker has traversed the southwest border-country and the high moorland commons to the Drivage Bottom tunnel, has entered the Forest and looked upon Foxtor Mire spread below the southern hill-chain, and crossed the west side of the central basin. He can now see the sterner threshold of north Dartmoor, although the headwaters of the Devonport leat are by no means as distant as these lonely fenlands; the three valleys of its source are amazingly contrasted and exemplify one of Dartmoor's most compelling attributes – its scenic variety.

On approaching the B3357 highway at Ockery Bridge, notice the outline of a small plat, the scant foundations of the cottage that once stood here and a short lane leading to the clapper bridge. The fenced area on the opposite (left) bank of the brook contains the prison sewage works. Cross the road and view the leat passing through the prison grounds; a large clapper bridge of three openings spans the brook and, beyond it, a finely built granite aqueduct carries the foul leat to the sewage works. A copse blocks the further view upstream, but the prison authorities have kindly allowed the author to follow the leat.

Beyond the aqueduct is another clapper, of two openings, where new imposts have been laid upon original piers and which is likely to have been built during the war-prison years (1809–15). Entering the copse, the leat passes below a road from the prison buildings to the farmlands; in this reach it is accompanied on its higher side by a dry, parallel channel, which could well represent the earliest attempt to leat water to the war prison before the cutting of the larger capacity Prison Leat from the River Walkham. Beyond the farm-road bridge is the aqueduct carrying water from the Cowsic and West Dart branches of the Devonport leat; passing across the brook, therefore, the water joins the Blacka Brook branch near the farm-road bridge. The Blacka Brook headweir, meanwhile, 300yd (274m) upstream from the aqueduct, is of interest in being the original one of 1794, pre-dating the two eastern branch-leats. The traveller John Andrews wrote of the Blacka Brook intake in 1794 (*Transactions of the Devonshire Association* 73, 1941): 'Water to go to Dock is taken from Blacka Brook about a Mile west of Two Bridges: some miles of it are completed.' The headweir, sited obliquely to ensure a moderate continuity of flow for the brook, is a wide, well-built structure of granite; the entire scheme was completed, of course, some years before the war prison was built and the ground enclosed.

Cowsic branch
From the Blacka Brook aqueduct, the Cowsic leat runs due east through the prison lands below Waldron (ie the prison farm),

before contouring the southwest spur of Omen Beam. The walker should join it at 603751 where it passes obliquely beneath the B3357 highway on Beardown Hill, as the road here is locally called. Mount the (north) roadside stile and follow the channel along the flank of Omen Beam, passing the point where the water emerges by gravity from the Cowsic aqueduct in the valley below. Walk always on the left bank; at a later stage in the walk, it is well worth deviating to examine the splendid granite aqueduct built in 1898, which carries the West Dart branch of the leat (see cover picture). Continue along the Cowsic branch path; red military warning flags flying from tors and hills need not deter the walker provided he keeps strictly to the leatside path, which lies always outside the range area. Recently when walking this portion of the leat I met four wader-clad watermen, one pushing a wheelbarrow *in* the leat because, he explained, it was easier than negotiating the narrow leatside path! The volume of water here is naturally less than before the (Cowsic) aqueduct was built and the entire West Dart intake joined that of the Cowsic. Pass a flood-relief sluice and channel and notice two hunting gates above the opposite bank, near the plantations.

On nearing the headweir, the fine tor of Beardown (north) rises to the right and Lydford Tor beyond. Further up the Cowsic valley appears Conies Down marked by its diminutive tor. A small bridge and meter-house stand near the weir, where impressive masonry of 1794 can be seen, with approach steps. A clam spans the river and large flagstones have been laid in the bed below the weir to counteract the erosive force of the river's current.

West Dart branch

Twelve yards (11m) upstream from the Cowsic weir, the West Dart branch once entered the river, the combined flow providing a large intake at the weir. Cross the clam and examine the point of entry, where a flood-relief sluice and channel still remain; the overgrown, long-disused channel leads away from the old entry point along the Beardown valley-side and into the plantation, where it cannot be followed, and emerges from the dark, coniferous density above the river's left bank near several rabbit buries of the old Beardown sporting warren; these are marked on OS maps in Gothic lettering as 'pillow mounds', but they date only from the closing years of the eighteenth century.

The Cowsic aqueduct is easily reached by walking upstream from Beardown Bridge and is set in a pleasant scene opening into the central basin. In the old (dry) channel above, some slab-lining remains, but beyond a broken cart clapper the channel is an open, green ditch; reaching a steep-bedded streamlet rising among the Beardown trees, the high-level approach of the channel makes it virtually certain to have been aqueducted across this, slabs being positioned to resist erosion of the bed at the downstream end (of the aqueduct), which probably was a simple, oaken conduit. Mr A. Forbes of Beardown Farm has kindly allowed me to follow this portion of the leat in order to record it, but it must be emphasised that **there is no right of way** between its emergence from the plantation and the syphon pipe that conducts flowing water to the Cowsic aqueduct. The walker who has visited the aqueduct must then follow the Beardown farm road to the spur of the hill where the leat flows near the plantation. It is permissible to follow it downstream to the syphon pipe, from where the channel may be viewed passing through the private farm fields. The syphon pipe and aqueduct of 1898, of course, obviated the continuing maintenance of more than a mile of channel to the Cowsic headweir.

Now turn about and follow the leat UP. Walk outside the wire fence and enter the east stand of the plantations, where a fine view is seen over the central basin to the southern heights. Mount the stile (Dartmoor National Park Authority yellow-spot route) and continue along the left bank. About 100yd (91m) from the stile a green way approaches the right bank through the trees, but its continuation below the leat has been overplanted; a curved wall and some masonry here suggest the former existence of a bridge to carry the track. Beyond this, a wide spillway releases flood water into a very deep gully, with remaining slotted granite posts for the former sluice that controlled the flow.

On emerging from the plantations at a stile, a delightful picture is presented of Crockern Farm nestling in the West Dart valley backed by Crockern Tor. A short way from the stile an old farm track crosses the leat and Littaford and Longaford

Tors are glimpsed ahead. The path is wide, the walking easy and the view of the West Dart valley pleasant. Leap-stones occur and the channel is substantially banked as it contours two re-entrants. A clapper has been laid across the channel where this appears to have been narrowed for the purpose. Beyond the second re-entrant is a small footbridge, and some massive bedrock where an old wall pre-dated the cutting of the leat – though perhaps only by fifteen years or so, as it may have been a part of the original enclosure made in 1780 by John Hannaford for Edward Bray of Tavistock, the builder of Beardown Farm.

The military range warning-board is intended only to deter walkers from climbing Beardown when firing is in progress, as the course of the leat here is also outside the range. The river glistens below, a hunting gate and ford appear, the scenery becomes wilder and makes a splendid setting for the primeval oak forest of Wistmans, now appearing below on the river's left bank (Pl. 2). Beardown has a distinct scarp falling to the right bank where the river rushes noisily over stickles. Opposite the central grove of the wood (there are three) is another range-board, a watermen's hut stands beside the leat and a clapper bridge opposite the north grove.

The river makes a considerable fall downstream from the headweir and it comes as a surprise when walking still 50ft (15m) above it, to see the weir just ahead. Weir, spillway and

Plate 2   Devonport Leat in West Dart Valley: The continuing line is seen on the further hillside (Beardown). Longaford Tor rises above the east valley-side and the primeval oak wood of Wistmans is spread below

Plate 3   Devonport Leat – West Dart Headweir: The fine workmanship of the 1790s is apparent. The water is captured in its transitional passage between upper and middle reaches

associated masonry exhibit fine workmanship (Pl. 3); the river, swift and prone to vagaries in flow, must have been diverted for the work to be carried out, and a dry, narrow channel is seen on the left bank. Longaford is the nearest tor on the ridge eastward, whilst Beardown (north) rises west of the river. It certainly is worth climbing to the tor *when no red flags are flying* to see the fine view: directly north is Dart Hole, tributary valley of Methern Brook, with a tinners' leat on the west bank and the rocks of Crow and Rough Tors above (both are pronounced to rhyme with 'cow'); the Lych Way is visible making a gradual, oblique descent of the east valley-side to the hunting gate above Wistmans Wood Ford, where it crosses the river and ascends through a gully to the north plain of Beardown, there to pass Lydford Tor en route for Travellers' Ford on the River Cowsic. Near the ancient track at the north extremity of Wistmans Wood are rabbit buries and the foundations of the small wooden house of the former Wistmans Wood (sporting) Warren. Higher Whiten Tor rises north of Longaford and the domed Wildbanks Hill above the river's upper reach – a scene providing an altogether magnificent moorland climax to the retracing of the remarkable 'Dock Leat' from the built-up areas of the modern city of Plymouth.

2
Grimstone and Sortridge Leat

7 miles (11.3km)   Map 2

Historical digest
In view of the antiquity of the manor houses and farms that
are the main terminals of this leat, it is likely to have originated
not less than five centuries ago – and possibly even earlier. The
leat, taken from the River Walkham opposite the foot of Great
Mis Tor, passes through enclosed lands of Whitchurch parish
and returns to the river in the border-country. Bull's-eye stones
and delivery points are more numerous than on any other
Dartmoor leat; indeed, so great is the reliance placed upon the
leat that any interference with the water on the high moor,
especially during a period of dry weather, results in barely a
trickle reaching the actual terminals.

The leat provides a highly scenic walk in which the wild and
rugged country at the source is progressively exchanged for the
gentle undulations and soft, pastel colours and woodlands of the
lower Walkham valley, and the wide waters of the Tavy and
Tamar estuaries backed by the Cornish moors. Industry, past
and present, is much in evidence in Walkham country, where
tin has been won and smelted in medieval blowing houses, and
in later years taken to Cornwall for smelting; and where huge
quantities of peat have been transported by packhorses from the
upper reach peat-beds to Mary Tavy, Peter Tavy and
Tavistock. Granite has been quarried at the nineteenth-century
workings of Foggin Tor, Swell Tor, King Tor, Ingra Tor,
Feather, Heckwood and Pu Tors, as it is to this day at the works
of the Merivale Granite Company; also granite quarried on the
east slopes of the valley was transported to Plymouth by rail
along the circuitous P&DR of 1823 (see p15) and its successor the
GWR (1873–1956), the latter appearing from the leat as a line
drawn round the spur of King Tor. There is history, too, at the
crossing by the leat of two ancient trans-Dartmoor packhorse
tracks linking the eastern border-country towns of Chagford
and Ashburton with Tavistock.

As so often with Dartmoor leats, we have to consider not one channel but several. The parallel, dry leat originating at a higher intake on the river and joining the flowing channel on Barn Hill near Windypost Cross was cut, according to Mr Sid Warren of Peter Tavy, at the time when William Duke (*c*1876) began to develop his Tor Quarry workings on a commercial scale, in order to avoid interference with the water at the works (*cf* p17–19). The lengthy diversion channel is stated by Sid Warren to have raised such effective opposition among the commoners whose flocks grazed the area that it proved to be abortive.

That this disused channel did carry water for some time, however, is proved by the presence of a link channel between it and the Grimstone leat south of the highway; by two large clapper cart-bridges on the lower south slope of Little Steeple Tor which would have been in use when heavy paving setts cut on the slopes of the tors were carted down to the road en route for Tavistock before Tor Quarry was opened; and by a water-worn channel beyond the site of the aqueduct across Beckamoor Combe (north of the highway) where embankments were constructed at either end of the launder.

Following the leat (DOWN)

A car may be parked in the large space on the north roadside, west of Merivale, at 530750. Walk over the open moor along the east flank of the Steeple Tors ridge above the quarry workings, by following the channel of the disused diversion leat. Pass above the newtake of Shillapark Farm. The head of the Grimstone leat will eventually appear below, opposite the foot of Great Mis Tor.

A small island of irregular shape lies in the river at the west-southwest foot (553774) of Great Mis Tor; 100yd (91m) below the island is the weir for the leat intake. A straight, well-cut channel (right bank) initiates the flow and the leat quickly gains height above the steeply falling river. An ancient crossing-place on the river with good approaches, just below the headweir, could well have been a tinners' ford. Visible from the leat are the tors of Over, Foggin, King and Little King backed by Sharp Tor and Peak Hill. Look upstream and notice the commencement of the diversion channel (which has guided

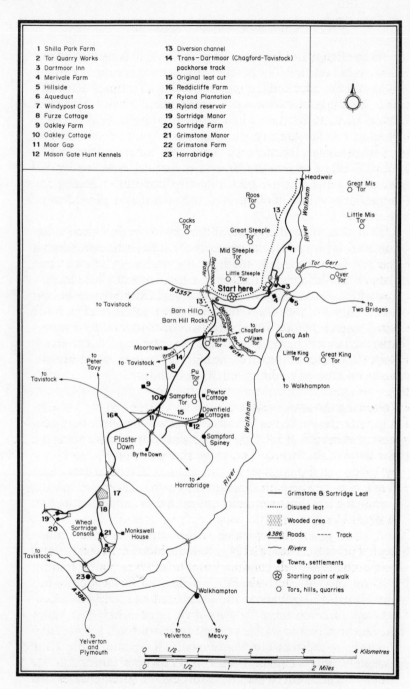

1 Shilla Park Farm
2 Tor Quarry Works
3 Dartmoor Inn
4 Merivale Farm
5 Hillside
6 Aqueduct
7 Windypost Cross
8 Furze Cottage
9 Oakley Farm
10 Oakley Cottage
11 Moor Gap
12 Mason Gate Hunt Kennels
13 Diversion channel
14 Trans—Dartmoor (Chagford-Tavistock) packhorse track
15 Original leat cut
16 Reddicliffe Farm
17 Ryland Plantation
18 Ryland reservoir
19 Sortridge Manor
20 Sortridge Farm
21 Grimstone Manor
22 Grimstone Farm
23 Horrabridge

Headweir
Great Mis Tor
Little Mis Tor
Roos Tor
Cocks Tor
Great Steeple Tor
Mid Steeple Tor
Little Steeple Tor
Over Tor
Over Tor Gert
River Walkham
Beckamoor Water
B 3357
to Tavistock
Start here
to Two Bridges
Barn Hill
Barn Hill Rocks
to Chagford
Long Ash
Vixen Tor
Little King Tor
Great King Tor
Moortown
Feather Tor
(track)
to Tavistock
to Peter Tavy
to Walkhampton
Pu Tor
Sampford Tor
Pewtor Cottage
to Tavistock
Downfield Cottages
Sampford Spiney
Plaster Down
By the Down
to Horrabridge
River Walkham
Wheal Sortridge Consols
Monkswell House
to Tavistock
Walkhampton
to Yelverton and Plymouth
to Yelverton
to Meavy

Grimstone & Sortridge Leat
.... Disused leat
Wooded area
A386 Roads ---- Track
Rivers
● Towns, settlements
✪ Starting point of walk
○ Tors, hills, quarries

0   1/2   1   2   3   4 Kilometres
0   1/2   1   2 Miles

Map 2 showing Walk 2 Grimstone and Sortridge Leat

the walker from the roadside) and the large Bronze Age hut villages on Claytor Moor and Langstone Moor beyond.

The leat, in places high-banked, flows for a mile (1.6km) before entering the outermost newtake of Shillapark; near the north boundary wall a clapper cart-bridge carries a track from the farm to the much-used Mistor Ford on the river. The huge tor itself assumes from this distance an individual aura of majesty denied to many a higher mountain; the dense clitter of Roos Tor above the west valley-side thins out (which was fortunate for the leat-builders) and an isolated, ruined hut circle appears below the left bank.

The Grimstone leat now enters the newtake, where **there is no right of way.** The walker should follow the higher boundary of the newtake to the point where the leat emerges near the farm entrance and the Merivale track continues towards the quarry. It now passes below the clitters of Great and Mid Steeple Tors; on the slope of the ridge, paving setts were once cut and shaped by workmen kneeling at diminutive benches known as 'bankers', numerous examples of which remain above the leat. Below the left bank are the remains of an early nineteenth-century tin mine recorded as Wheal *Fortune* – an optimistic label that brought its promoters as little prosperity as that experienced by the Eva family at the contemporary Wheal *Lucky* near Rundlestone. The channel that supplied the mine waterwheel branched from the Grimstone leat, an arrangement presumably agreed upon by the parties concerned.

The Merivale-Shillapark road runs through the quarry works and is a permissible path for walkers; to remain on the actual course of the leat, however, here well above the road, call at the quarry office and ask permission of the manager, Mr Fred Pote. The channel passes through a rockfield – the lower edge of the Steeple Tors clitter – into a large (disused) oblong reservoir, from where branch channels conduct water to delivery points below including the old Merivale Post Office, now 'Tor Cottage', where there still remains a red telephone kiosk and the Dartmoor Inn (via a branch bull's-eye). The flow is now piped through the hillside and cascades to the works level, where it once drove a waterwheel, and later a turbo-generator; here it is again piped and emerges south of the works buildings to continue on a lower level, first through a granite-covered conduit, then an open one. The former Methodist chapel here was a school for the quarrymen's children – from Merivale Cottages, demolished about thirty years ago – and was attended by Mr Warren's mother. Merivale granite from the great Tor Quarry now travels to many parts of the kingdom, much of it to London for building, and travellers on the B3357 highway pass directly below the looming waste-tips.

The leat passes beneath the quarry road where this bends to join the highway, and beneath the latter through a granite conduit, from which it flows across Whitchurch Common near the Merivale newtake wall before bearing westward towards Beckamoor Combe. Follow the right bank; notice a former ford where erosion has been arrested by banking. A track from Sampford Spiney to the quarry crosses the leat on a clapper bridge. A good view of Vixen and Pu Tors now opens with the Beckamoor valley backed by Feather and Heckwood Tors. The modern OS version 'Pew' is unauthentic: Pu Tor and Putor Common appear on the OS 1809 one-inch map and the Sampford Spiney Tithe Map of 1844, and Great Pu Tor on the Whitchurch Tithe Map of 1843. The leat-side path passes through a rockfield nurturing two struggling thorn trees,

Plate 4   Grimstone and Sortridge Leat – Aqueduct over Beckamoor Water: Vixen Tor appears beyond the valley. Horizon (left to right): King Tor, Swell Tor, Leedon Tor, Ingra Tor (below horizon)

beyond which is a wide clapper cart-bridge carrying an old track from Whitchurch and Moortown to pits and workings on this granite-strewn land: sett-makers walking to their work on the Steeple Tors ridge would have found this a more convenient route than the bridge upstream leading to the main quarry. Stone pits, omnipresent on the common, now become even more numerous, some of them very large. Another bridge occurs, above which are the scant remains of a small longhouse with a curved passage on the west side. Continue across the base of a medieval wall and follow the leat along its high, curving approach to Beckamoor Combe. This is an altogether picturesque place overlooked by the crags and pinnacles of Walkham country's fine tors. The stream in the combe, Beckamoor Water, passes below a small concrete aqueduct carrying the leat (Pl. 4), which receives an affluent from the right bank upstream; this undertaking obviated a lengthy contour-loop in the valley. Beside the aqueduct a small notice-board carries this appeal: Please do not obstruct or interfere with this water supply.

On the flank of Barn Hill above the leat is the continuing channel of the diversion leat, which runs north of the highway, while the Grimstone leat crosses Whitchurch Common. Lying outside a ruined building (known as the Blacksmith's Shop) below the former, is a splendid wheelright's stone. On approaching Windypost Cross, the Longford channel curves slightly to join the Grimstone leat as this turns southwestward down the hill.

As Beckamoor Combe opens below Beckamoor Ford, a ruined tinners' house appears on the right bank of the brook. An ancient way from Tavistock to the Walkham valley tin-works crosses the stream beside two Sampford Spiney bond-stones, visible on the further bank. The leat now gains the crest of the west valley-side at the fine old Windypost Cross (Pl. 5). The ridge here is crossed by the trans-Dartmoor (Chagford-Tavistock) track which, west of Merivale, combines with the Tavistock-Ashburton track crossing Beckamoor Water at Feathertor Ford. A bull's-eye occurs in the leat here, admitting water into a branch channel serving Pu Tor ('Pewtor') Cottage and points near Sampford Spiney. This branch channel was actually the original leat; the present main channel flowing at

Plate 5   Grimstone and Sortridge Leat at Windypost Cross: The controlling bull's-eye stone lies in the channel near the cross. The original channel, now the Pu Tor branch, is extreme right and the modern main channel behind the cross. The line of the pre-turnpike Chagford–Tavistock track crosses the leat near the bull's-eye stone. On the horizon are (left) Great Steeple Tor and (right) Great Mis Tor

the west foot of Pu Tor was not cut until between 1873–80, and was undertaken by John Henry Hearn of Oakley Farm and neighbouring farmers whose water supply from other sources was wholly inadequate. These enterprising men therefore cut the leat from Windypost Cross to Moor Gap and inserted bull's-eye stones – 'inch-holes' as the moormen call them – to feed branches to their farms and cottages; Mr John Hearn of Oakley Cottage recalls that an agreement had to be reached by his grandfather with the mine owners of Sortridge Consols before the work commenced.

To deal first with the branch channel; crossing the Heckwood-Pu Tors col, it descends to Pewtor Cottage and is now in places a small channel only a few inches in width as it continues towards Downfield Cottages under Little Pu Tor (locally 'Sampford' Tor). The cottages occupy a plot marked on the Whitchurch Tithe Map of 1843 as '2 arable fields'. The water then passes beneath the Sampford Spiney road and runs westward near its south verge to supply the Spooners and West Dartmoor Hunt kennels at Mason Gate, from where it descends through farm fields to Watery Ford and the mother stream below. It should be understood that the channel below the road is a branch of the original leat which can easily be traced on the *north* roadside as it leaves Downfield Cottages, except for a short length obliterated in the construction of the vehicular access road to the rear of the cottages; below this it is visible as a grassy ditch. Reaching an ancient, small enclosure opposite the hunt kennels at Mason Gate, it occupies the actual cornditch of the enclosure, which has been deepened to maintain the leat's gravity flow at the higher corner. The water continued through the ditch to the northwest corner, from where it is clearly defined as – again parallel with the road at a distance of about 100yd (91m) – it runs across the bracken-infested common below Sampford Tor to the Moortown road. There are no signs that any bridge stood here, and the road probably crossed the leat at a ford. The channel then bends to follow the road to the junction known as Moor Gap, where it passed through a duct beneath the Whitchurch road and now receives water from the existing main channel cut by John Henry Hearn and his neighbours.

Now to return to Windypost Cross: this striking viewpoint includes much of the splendid Walkham torscape, Tavistock in the vale of Tavy, Bodmin Moor beyond and the southwest in-country undulating gently to the twin estuaries of Tavy and Tamar and the English Channel. The present-day main leat descends southwest from the moorland escarpment to Plaster Down, passing en route more Sampford Spiney bond-stones (all engraved SP). John Henry Hearn's bull's-eye stones, counting that at the Windypost as first in the series, are as follows: second, a branch to the Moortown enclosures; third, to Furze Cottage and Langstone; fourth, to Oakley Cottage and Farm; and fifth, on reaching Plaster Down to Reddicliff Farm. Below Windypost Cross the leat runs for a short way beside the old Chagford packhorse track and, as the leat diverges to flow southward, the view is worthy of attention. Prowtytown Rocks rise beyond the Moortown enclosures; a large expanse of east Cornwall is visible and the mass of Cocks Tor dominates in the north beyond Barn Hill Rocks, with Great Steeple Tor northeastward. The gradient steepens under Pu Tor, and a collapsed impost of a fine clapper bridge of the 1870s has deflected the water, which has itself excavated an adequate diversion channel. A quarrymen's path from the Horrabridge-Plaster Down area climbs the hill and fords the leat. The small weir and bull's-eye stone (fourth in the series) above Oakley Cottage lie at the foot of Sampford Tor, the stones from which they were cut being on the right bank. This delightful vale, with the sparkling leat a silver ribbon threading emerald-green verdure, lichen-spotted rocks, distant views and the overshadowing Pu and Sampford Tors, is an ideal place to take the oldest and youngest members of the family for a breath of Dartmoor air and a peaceful, carefree environment.

Near Moor Gap, another bull's-eye controls a branch supply to 'By the Down'; beyond this at Moor Gap (524729), the leat passes beneath the Sampford road through a long, tarmac-surfaced clapper, and under the opposite hedge is a Sampford Spiney-Tavistock bond-stone marked $\frac{SS}{T}$. Follow the leat to a wide ford near the cornditch wall, left; beyond this, on Plaster Down, a granite slab remains in position as the likely relic of a former bridge beside a pool and another ford. The numerous fords on this stretch of the leat are due to the comparative shallowness of the channel on the level plain, so facilitating fording. The road crossing the leat at 523728 is on the line of the Buckfast-Tavistock monastic way, here passing between Huckworthy Cross, Warrens Cross and Pixies' Cross on Whitchurch Down. Under a cornditch wall beside this road is a Whitchurch parish bond-stone marked 'WB'. Another bull's-eye stone, eighth on the overall course of the leat so far, controls the branch channel to Reddicliff Farm. Two more fords occur on either side of a low-lying, marshy tract – a skating rink in the winter of 1984–5 – before the leat makes a sharp southward bend just short of the Horrabridge road (the ancient highway from Plymouth to Okehampton via the Walkham bridge at Horrabridge, Moorshop and Harford Bridge, Tavy). Below the bend is an inscribed standing stone (see Fig 1). This, a milestone of the old Plymouth highway, was in all probability moved to its present position when the former Plaster Down military camp was constructed (it was demolished *c*1973).

Fig 1 Milestone of the old Plymouth highway

The southern end of Plaster Down is a pleasant greensward to reach which the leat passes beneath, first, a byroad to Walkhampton; second, the Horrabridge road, beside which is a small, triangular green bordered by enclosure walls and Ryland Plantation. The leat passes the relic of a former footbridge on the green and enters a stroll following the northwest wall of the plantation; a bridge to nowhere occurs here, as former access from it into the plantation enclosure is now blocked. Below the bridge, the leat has been lined over a length of 8ft (2.4m) and the channel divided by a low wall 9ft (2.7m) long; the right branch enters the Sortridge lands and the left supplies an open reservoir south of Ryland Plantation, originally built to supply the waterwheel of Sortridge Consols Mine, and continues to Grimstone. The Sortridge branch shortly reaches a gate, where the stroll narrows to a lane beside the leat leading to Sortridge Manor and Farm. **There is no right of way beyond the gate into Sortridge Lane nor into Ryland Plantation and the reservoir**; the gate is therefore the best place for the walker to leave the leat. This chapter ends with a short historical account of the terminals in the enclosed lands of the two manors and farms, to which **there is no public access.**

43

Grimstone Manor

From Ryland reservoir a branch channel carries water to Monkswell House, while the main channel falls to Grimstone, where it passes through a large, walled garden to a delivery point at the former stables – now Grimstone Mews. Mr A. J. Whieldon, present occupant of the manor, has made attractive ornamental use of the water in his lower garden, favourable to bird and pond life, before it joins a stream known as Dosta Brook, descends to Horrabridge village beside the school and returns to the Walkham, its mother stream. Mr Whieldon has kindly allowed me to quote from an historical note he has prepared about the manor:

> The earliest history of Grimstone is in the Register of Bishop Stapledon of Exeter. Dated February 2, 1309, it stated: 'Licence to hear Divine Service in any decent Oratory at Grimstone with the rector's assent'. A domestic chapel was built and it is thought that a small stone shed in the grounds, now restored as a summer house, may have been that chapel. There was also mention in the Register of 'Petrum de Grymstone, clericum', Vicar of Broadclyst from 1326 to 1327 so there seems to have been an early connection with the Church . . . (In 1659) a schedule of title deeds relating to the Manor of 'Em Grimstone' was begun. On the estate were various houses known as Lower Grimstone (now Grimstone Farm), Rowe's Grimstone, Little Grimstone, Higher Grimstone and Teddy's Grimstone . . .

Grimstone Farm

It is interesting that the present tenant of the farm should be a Rowe (see quotation above) – Mr John Rowe. A branch channel from the leat supplied the farm by augmenting the flow from a spring in the fields. The branch is now disused, as the farm received the mains water-supply in 1963. The spring still flows, however, delivering water into a fine granite trough in the farm court. Until recent years, John Rowe and other recipients of the supply from the main leat worked together in a biannual clearing and repairing of the channel, but it seems that this concerted effort has now given way to a less organised style of leat maintenance.

Sortridge Consols Mine (opened primarily to mine copper)

The former mine-captain's house, occupied and now named

'Avondale', stands high above the Horrabridge-Whitchurch road, and the wheel-pit to which water was leated from Rylands reservoir is now infilled. The mine ceased work for some years in 1868, when among the items placed on sale was a 24ft (7.3m) waterwheel; another, the last waterwheel to be worked by the Rylands branch of the leat, was installed in 1883, when a serious accident occurred in which the mine-captain named Williams, and Newcombe a miner, were drowned in a flooded level. Production figues for 1856–9 were 4,302 tons of copper, sold for £28,578.

Sortridge Manor
This fine Tudor house was built in 1558 by John Skerrett, a churchwarden of St Eustace, Tavistock. Alice, daughter of John Skerrett, married Judge Glanville of Kilworthy; she inherited the manor in 1615 and, following the death of her husband, married Sir Francis Godolphin. The leat, having for many centuries served the two historic manors and some distinguished occupants, passes by the north end of the house and through the fields below to return to the river.

Sortridge Farm
The leat water enters a long granite trough in the farm court, inscribed 'DG 1661'; nearby is another large trough inscribed 'IG 1667'. The water supply was conveniently accessible to the servants at the manor, where the kitchen door opened onto the court.

3
Devon Wheal Friendship Leat

4.5 miles (7.2km)   Map 3

Historical digest

A leat having the function, shared only by one other major leat and a few minor streams, of supplying seventeen waterwheels (in 1875) will be an impressive stream capable of delivering an unfailing head of water to working points: such is the main Wheal Friendship channel. Its companion leat, taken in from the Tavy at Hill Bridge, is the subject of Chapter 4. Helen Harris (*Industrial Archaeology of Dartmoor*) states that eight of the wheels were for pumping, the largest being 51 feet in diameter with 10 foot breast; four others of rather smaller diameter operated crushers and stamping-mills. An 80-in cylinder steam engine stood in reserve for times when water supplies ran low.

White's Directory of Devon for 1878–9 gives James Jenkins as manager and purser of Wheal Friendship, and James Tredenick as the mine agent. The leat, recorded as being in use as early as 1824 and shown on the Mary Tavy Tithe Map of 1840, was engineered by the remarkable John Taylor, builder of the Tavistock Canal. It followed the contour of Kingsett Down and discharged its burden into the upper valley of Cholwell Brook, from which the water was taken as required by numerous leats for the several waterwheels. Additional branches, also constructed by Taylor, conveyed water to the Wheal Betsy silver and lead mine (see p51); and to Black Down Mine (503806), the channel crossed by the A386 road at Barrett's Bridge. Production figures for Wheal Friendship published in Dines's *The Metalliferous Mining Region of South-west England* are:

Good dividends paid before 1790

1800–65	162 tons of black tin	1908–9	42,900 oz silver
–85	155,099 tons of copper		6,940 tons pyrites
	1,170 tons of lead		160 tons zinc ore

46

The leat has two remarkable features, one illusory and one substantial: first, the optical illusion, so well known to Dartmoor walkers, of water flowing uphill between Nattor and Kingsett Downs; second, the magnificent, at times awe-inspiring granite gorge known as Tavy Cleave. In order to introduce the reader to this extraordinary piece of English moorland, guidance begins with a loop-shaped walk designed to provide a striking view of the cleave and a safe descent to the leat below. This loop walk should not be attempted in misty conditions, nor is it suitable for young children; in such cases, substitute an out-and-back leatside walk from Lane End. *Warning: Willsworthy military range.*

Following the leat (DOWN)

Drive from Mary Tavy (reached by the A386 road north from Tavistock) to Lane End; cross the cattle-grid and park beside the military flagpole at 537823.

Walk towards Ger Tor at the head of the down. Cross the leat bridge; remain on the track until near the hill-crest, then make for a clear, grassy path near rocks; bear right towards the main pile of the tor. Look down from the northeast side at the grandeur of the scene; from the southeast side view the leat flowing from the headweir.

Do not yet descend to the valley floor, but cross Tavy Cleave Plains by making towards the cone of Hare Tor; notice the hut circles of an early Bronze Age settlement below, right. Descend to these, cross a streamlet falling to the river and walk to the broken pile of Tavy Cleave Sharp. Look through a narrow gap between the tor rocks to the river below: the view is memorable. Return to a lower point on the tributary streamlet and make for the valley floor as the difficult ground allows; follow a rough path, right, to the leat headweir.

The volume of water taken in here greatly depletes the river in periods of drought. Follow the leatside path, which leads out of the granite fastness of the cleave towards the more open valley of the border-country Tavy. The rapid gain in height of leat over river is due to the consistently steep fall of the latter over a never-ending series of steps; falling 1,000ft (305m) in under 7 miles it is Britain's second swiftest river after the Spey of the Cairngorms. Beyond the sharp bend of the channel below

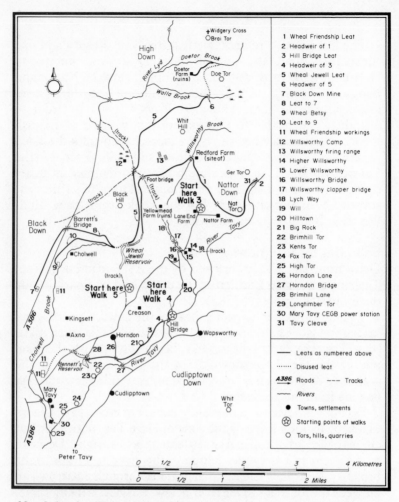

Key to numbered features on map:

1 Wheal Friendship Leat
2 Headweir of 1
3 Hill Bridge Leat
4 Headweir of 3
5 Wheal Jewell Leat
6 Headweir of 5
7 Black Down Mine
8 Leat to 7
9 Wheal Betsy
10 Leat to 9
11 Wheal Friendship workings
12 Willsworthy Camp
13 Willsworthy firing range
14 Higher Willsworthy
15 Lower Willsworthy
16 Willsworthy Bridge
17 Willsworthy clapper bridge
18 Lych Way
19 Will
20 Hilltown
21 Big Rock
22 Brimhill Tor
23 Kents Tor
24 Fox Tor
25 High Tor
26 Horndon Lane
27 Horndon Bridge
28 Brimhill Lane
29 Longtimber Tor
30 Mary Tavy CEGB power station
31 Tavy Cleave

──── Leats as numbered above
.... Disused leat
A386 Roads   ─── Tracks
∿∿ Rivers
● Towns, settlements
⊛ Starting points of walks
○ Tors, hills, quarries

Map 3 showing Walk 3 Devon Wheal Friendship Leat; Walk 4 Hill Bridge Leat; Walk 5 Wheal Jewell Leat

Nat Tor and its clitter, where a bridge spans the leat, Nattor Farm and Nattor Down come into view. A branch channel conducts water to the farm and a flood-relief sluice heads a channel that follows the outer wall of Nattor Newtake and returns to the river. Above the river's left bank rises the massive Standon Hill, whilst ahead the curving moorland traces the lower, more gentle lines of Gibbet Hill, Black Down and Whit Hill.

48

The walker will shortly reach the timber bridge crossed at the start of the walk and will see the flagpole, parked car(s) and Lane End. From the bridge is visible the modern terminal of the leat at the Wheal Jewell reservoir; despite the contrary impression, the water must continue to flow downhill to arrive there for, as already explained, the flow of a leat is maintained by gravity alone. Other features seen from the bridge are the fields of old Yellowmead (west of Lane End Farm), the Lych Way crossing the leat and ascending to Forstall Cross, the Willsworthy Camp shooting butts, the site and old enclosures of Redford, and the Dartmoor Path crossing the south flank of Whit Hill.

Considerable ground drainage enters the leat from Nattor Down and several flood-relief sluices and channels occur, with an actual weir for the Redford overflow. The old farm, demolished in the early years of this century, was, wrote Eden Phillpotts in *The Whirlwind*, driven like a wedge into the stony wilderness beneath Dartmoor's north-western ramparts (Pl. 6). An old military target railway, most of its rails remaining *in situ*, may be seen beyond the east enclosure wall of the farm.

The leat now passes under Whit Hill, where the illusion of its uphill flow returns in strength. Footbridges occur above and below Redford and medieval (and later) walls in the area are numerous, one being bisected by the leat at the upper bridge. A modern vehicular bridge also spans the channel under Whit Hill. Reaching the hill-crest at Forstall Cross, right, the leat crosses both the Dartmoor Path and the Wheal Jewell leat (Walk 5), which is here converging on the Wheal Friendship channel.

The walker following the leat on the flank of Black Hill will see a splendid view of the western escarpment. A short way ahead on Kingsett Down is the conning tower-like control-house for the reservoir; two stones stand together on the down between the twin leats, one unmarked, the other inscribed 'WD 44', ie War Department range boundary-stone 44. A hill summit hundreds of feet above the in-country appears to be an unusual site for a gravity-fed reservoir, and, on looking back towards Ger Tor, the walker will still be deluded into believing that the water has all along flowed uphill to this point. He must, nevertheless, be told that he is here standing 95ft (30m) *below* the Tavy valley floor at Headweir! The standard of surveying needed to achieve this finely graded gravitational flow by engineers of the late eighteenth century, is impressive indeed.

The curvature of the reservoir helps to mitigate its concrete intrusion into the moorland scene (Pl. 7). Its function is to impound and deliver the leat water to Mary Tavy power station (Central Electricity Generating Board); this supplies current to the National Grid but can be switched to local use in case of emergency and is the largest hydro-electric scheme in England today. The water is not a domestic supply and, after powering the turbines, returns to the river.

As the leat approaches the reservoir, an old, dry branch channel leads off across the down, right; this carried the original supply to Black Down Mine (see p46). There is also a sluice-controlled branch channel, left, which conducts surplus water to the Hill Bridge leat (Walk 4). The leat is then joined by the Wheal Jewell channel, the original function of which was to turn the waterwheels of Wheal Jewell; but its site is now occupied by the reservoir and the extension reservoir – a large, walled and banked depression (as yet empty) – on its west side.

Plate 6   Wheal Friendship Leat at Redford: The leat (right) approaches the old enclosures. The site of the farm is in the lower left corner. On the horizon are (left) Little Hare Tor and Hare Tor and (right) the hill known as Palmer's Newtake

Plate 7   Wheal Jewell Reservoir – Kingsett Down: Here are impounded the waters of the Wheal Friendship and Wheal Jewell leats before being piped to the Mary Tavy CEGB hydro-electric power station. Horizon (left to right): Arms Tor, Brai Tor, Little Links Tor, Great Links Tor, Lydford Sharp Tor, Little Hare Tor, Hare Tor

The original Wheal Friendship channel curved westward on approaching Wheal Jewell and began a steep descent to the valley of Cholwell Brook, the augmented flow of which in mining days provided a perpetual supply for numerous leats. The leat also branched to the very successful, early nineteenth century mine of Wheal Betsy (510813) on the west valley-side of Cholwell Brook, where lead, copper, arsenic and silver were produced in varying quantities until the mine closed in 1877. The old engine house – the only one of its type remaining on the high moor – is a picturesque, if stark, reminder of the human skills and labour expended in the search for Dartmoor ore 150 years ago. It is a landmark familiar to travellers on the A386 highway crossing Black Down, which provides a convenient approach to the mine for motoring walkers, and there are numerous parking places nearby on the west roadside.

Water from the mine wheels returned to the brook to provide a maximum head for the several Wheal Friendship leats below. The southernmost working of the huge Wheal Friendship complex is now the site of the Mary Tavy power station, from which Cholwell Brook water again was extracted to supplement the supply from the Hill Bridge leat (Walk 4).

51

4
Hill Bridge Leat

1½ miles (2.4km)   Map 3

Historical digest
In a remote area of the west border-country, the River Tavy
passes beneath its first road bridge (533804) between the
hamlets of Willsworthy and Wapsworthy, the suffix of each
name underlining the Saxon origin of the valley-side farming
enclosures here that so readily reveal their antiquity to the eye.
For centuries – perhaps since Saxon times – a clapper bridge has
borne the valley settlers across the often tempestuous Tavy, and
here, if stepping stones upstream were dangerously awash,
passed those solemn cortèges of medieval times when the
moormen of the central basin bore their dead along the Lych
Way to Lydford St Petrock for burial. The (public) field path
descending to the river's left bank is that very track, its
continuation above the right bank now the basis of the
serpentine tarmac road ascending to Willsworthy.

The bridge in this deep valley, well named 'Hill' Bridge is, as
successor to the last (nineteenth-century) clapper, aesthetically
unworthy of its beautiful setting. Below it is a salmon ladder
and the headweir of the large-capacity leat that once conveyed
water to the south area of the Wheal Friendship mining
complex. An iron ladder set in the roadside bank gives access
from bridge to headweir, and the leatside path is for some way
open to public access. Beyond Brimhill Lane the water is now
diverted to a reservoir, from which it is piped to the hydro-
electric power station at Mary Tavy and thence returns to the
river via the tributary Cholwell Brook. The power station
receives from the three leats – Wheal Friendship, Hill Bridge,
Wheal Jewell – the surprising amount of 8,000 million gallons
(35m litres) a year.

Following the leat (DOWN)
There is space on the river's left bank near Hill Bridge to park a
car close beside the riverside wall. Cross the bridge and descend

52

the iron ladder. Follow the left bank of the leat throughout the walk. A large iron grating prevents driftwood from entering the channel, which immediately flows through a glade of great scenic charm – especially in springtime, when a wonderful start to the walk is provided by wild flowers, glimpses of Bagga Tor and Standon through burgeoning foliage, entire symphonies of bird-song and the rugged bed of the river below. Several flood-relief channels occur and an affluent cascading into the leat's right bank is the overflow channel from the Wheal Friendship leat mentioned on page 51.

A concrete bridge between field paths is succeeded by another cascading affluent under the rocky hillside, right. This soon becomes higher and the left bank steeper (where pipes have been inserted to aid flood-relief) as the leat enters Creason Wood. There is enchantment in this ancient woodland of time- and storm-battered oaks with twisted trunks and limbs swathed in epiphytes. The hillside above the leat is spattered by the clitter of an almost totally disintegrated tor; Tavy is wild and noisy in the valley below; and fat trout, disturbed by the leatside walker, dart through the water. This pleasing scene is backed by Cudlipptown Down, its bulk rising to 800ft (244m) above the east valley-side. Rock has been blasted, in at least one place, to make passage for the leat – a task well within the experience and expertise of the Wheal Friendship miners who undertook it; and a concrete footbridge has been placed to allow today's maintenance men to reach the right bank and remove fallen rocks from the leat.

At the south end of Creason Wood a huge crag towers above the leat; locally known as 'Big Rock', this forms a dramatic climax to the glen upstream. As the land assumes a more gentle aspect, a granite clapper bridge links steep field paths above and below the leat. The relatively open character of the country here allows one to appreciate how deeply Tavy has excavated the border-slates of its valley, creating a short secondary gorge. An overflow sluice and another clapper soon follow, and the Peter Tavy-Hill Bridge road is seen on the east valley-side. Numerous concrete bridges and leatside stiles are encountered as the land becomes increasingly more level, though the field below the leat terminates abruptly on the brink of the river gorge.

The houses of Horndon now appear above the right-bank

fields and a gate opens into Horndon Lane, which is carried over the leat by a concrete bridge. On the south side of the lane appears the sign KEEP OUT – PRIVATE C.E.G.B. (ie Central Electricity Generating Board), from which the walker may judge that, without prior permission from the superintendent engineer at the power station, he has **no right to proceed further along the leatside path.** This restriction, however, deprives him only of a comparatively short and unremarkable length of the leat as it crosses three or four farm fields with a clapper bridge in each, and where some fine old Devon hedges have been breached to allow of its construction.

The walker now has the choice of retracing the leatside path to Hill Bridge or following the road; to do this, descend Horndon Lane, cross the river at Horndon Bridge and turn left into the Peter Tavy-Hill Bridge road. To see two remaining features connected with the leat, however, drive across Hill Bridge and follow road signs to Mary Tavy, via Hill Town and Creason, to reach Horndon. Drive through the hamlet and park at 517801 opposite a signposted footpath through Brimhill Lane (left); follow the path and notice Boulters Tor on Smeardon Down and the massive Cudlipptown Down beyond the Tavy valley. Before rounding an abrupt bend to the southeast, look over a bridge parapet, left; a short length of dry leat channel is seen entering a tunnel (secreting a large pipe) beneath the lane. Walk round the bend and look over a gate, left; the flowing leat is here seen approaching through the (**no access**) farm fields south of Horndon Lane; the tunnel and bridge parapet show its original course to Friendship Mine, but this is now blocked by masonry and the flow diverted beneath Brimhill Lane beside the gate where the walker now stands; nearby are steps in the hedge once used to reach the leatside path. Now turn around and look over a wide gate in the opposite hedge at Bennett's reservoir, which is fed by the diverted leat, and to the left of it notice an embankment rounding the hill-spur above Kents Tor; although appearances suggest its origin as a tramroad level, it is merely the infilled trench for the pipeline now carrying water from reservoir to power station. The older excavation for the tunnel, driven by John Taylor in c1800 to obviate contouring the farmlands, has left a visible depression in the field between Brimhill Lane and

Midlands Farm; from there, the tunnel opened near Axna and delivered its flow to waterwheels and dressing-floors near Lane Head.

Return to the car. Drive past the 'Elephant's Nest' (OS maps still show the old name 'New Inn') to Mary Tavy, passing the mining works (right) to which the leat originally led. At the T-junction beside the school turn left; continue to keep left past the 'no through-road' sign and the church of St Mary to a wide turning space on the brink of the Tavy valley, where the road ends and it is possible to park without causing inconvenience to other drivers. This space occupies a spit of land between Tavy and the incoming Cholwell Brook, and under its west side is the hydro-electric power station which, built on the site of the former South Wheal Friendship, now receives the water piped from Bennett's reservoir.

Immediately below the parking space and within the power-station grounds are the masonry sides of a large waterwheel pit, to which water was delivered by a branch of the Hill Bridge leat; this descended through the fields above the church to reach the launder that formerly spanned the lane. The mine, which was also known as Wheal Ann, is recorded as having produced 7 tons of copper in 1824.

To round off a delightful expedition in the Dartmoor border-country, walk down the lane to Mary Tavy clam in yet another river glen, wild and unspoilt despite the proximity of mining remains, power station and – linked by lane and clam – the villages of Mary Tavy and Peter Tavy.

5
Wheal Jewell Leat

2.75 miles (4.4km)   Map 3

Historical digest
On Kingsett Down east of Black Down, at 523817, are the
mounds and pits of a spasmodic tin-mining venture. At work in
the eighteenth century, abandoned in 1797; re-opened in 1865;
it saw further bouts of industry in 1911 and 1924, when it was
worked for arsenic in conjunction with the Wheal Friendship
complex, having in 1916 adopted the group name, 'Wheal
Jewell and Mary Tavy Mine'. Ore raised at the mine was sent to
the dressing-floors of Wheal Friendship to be processed. There
are no records of output. Much of the mine's old surface
workings were obliterated in the construction of the 6 million
gallon (27.3m litres) reservoir in 1936–7, which then adopted the
name of the mine. A second, extension reservoir has since been
built (on the west side) on the site of the original mine reservoir,
further destroying the ground plan of leat, Wheal Jewell wheel-
pit and subsidiary channels. The leat, the work of John Taylor,
was cut in 1791 and now delivers an average of 2 million gallons
(9.1m litres) of water daily to Wheal Jewell reservoir, from
which it is piped to the Mary Tavy power station (see pp50, 51).

Following the leat (UP)
Drive from Lane Head, Mary Tavy, to Zoar (beyond
Horndon). Branch left at 523807 (beyond enclosures) into a
rough moorland road. Continue between enclosure walls ahead
and park on the open moor according to traffic regulations
within 15yd (14m) of the track. The building on the crest of the
down – architecturally so inappropriate to its position – is the
reservoir control-house. Walk to it, then along the bank of the
lozenge-shaped reservoir. A fine view is seen from here of the
moor's western escarpment, with Black Down, Gibbet Hill and
Brent Tor in the west. The leat and the nearby Wheal
Friendship channel (just below) now meet at the north end of

the reservoir, but the Jewell leat was formerly aqueducted across the larger channel, which here swings west to descend to the Cholwell Brook valley with a branch to Wheal Betsy (see p51).

Walk northward between the two flowing leats past two bond-stones on the summit of the down (see p49). The leats remain equidistant along the east flank of Black Hill; the old enclosures below, right, are those of the former Yellowmead Farm, through which a branch of the Lych Way runs from Willsworthy; nearer still, another track runs between the Yellowmead corndtich and the Friendship leat, a branch of the Lych Way from Hill Bridge via Snap Lane. The two branches unite a little beyond the west corndtich corner and mount the gentle slope to the Tavy-Lyd watershed at Willsworthy Camp. On the water-parting, leat, Dartmoor Path and Lych Way meet; before reaching this point, however, notice the acute eastward bend of the Friendship leat and the wooden footbridge spanning it; Lych Way is intersected by the leat at the bend and crosses the Wheal Jewell leat on a simple granite conduit to continue over the plain before descending towards Lydford. The Dartmoor Path, in passing from the Ring o' Bells cairn on Black Hill to the east flank of Whit Hill, also crosses the conduit, whilst the leat meanders across the plain to follow the west flank of the hill. Views from the plain are very striking, though not enhanced by the buildings and firing butts of the range. As the walker progresses, heights appear in the order (right to left) of Great Links Tor, Brai Tor, Arms Tor, Corn Ridge and Great Noddon and, a short way further, Hare Tor and the distant Sourton Tors. The Lych Way passes across the head valley of Sounscombe Brook, left, on its way to Down Lane Gate, and the blend of high moorland and Lyd border-country – Lydford's church and castle predominant above the village – is most attractive.

A short, higher, leat cut seems to have been made but abandoned in favour of the present one. As the channel bends in the direction of the Walla Brook valley, it has been banked with concrete blocks, no doubt the cheapest method, in today's economy, of counteracting erosion on bends. Barewalls Farm appears below, left, encircled by its windbreak of trees, and the leat intersects a corndtich wall, occupying the actual ditch for a short way on the downstream side. A tiny, single-storey stone house stands ahead, with a chimney and shuttered windows; designed with care to suit its environment, it is a military OP (observation post) – one of two such on the range – of pronounced architectural superiority to the concrete huts and tin shacks still seen in too many places on the moorland ranges. Beyond this delightful doll's house the leat obliquely intersects two more cornditches and brings into detailed view a wide range of the scenic attractions of Lyd country: the Walla Brook and Doe Tor Brook valleys under the impressive escarpment tors; the River Lyd twisting under Black Rock; the clear line of the Rattle Brook Peat Railway track passing through the cutting on Great Noddon; border-country villages, with Lydford central to this superb West Country panorama; and Brent Tor protruding against the distant Tamar valley backed by Bodmin Moor, with Brown Willy and Rough Tor visible on a clear day.

Numerous T-channels, cut by tinners to carry hillside drainage to workings on the valley floor, are intersected by the leat; tinners' leats that once took water from Walla Brook score the lower hillside. The sequestered ruin and green oasis of Doetor Farm (where the author drank tea beside the kitchen fire with Farmer and Mrs Ball over thirty years ago) soon appear on the plain between Doe Tor's foot and Walla Brook as the leat leaves the rounded flank of Whit Hill and heads towards the brook. Prominent on the smooth hillside above the leat is a cairn, nearest of several on the hill, containing the relic of a kistvaen consisting of one side- and two end-stones, although the OS marking is merely 'cairn'. A clapper cart-bridge of six imposts carries a track (a branch of the Dartmoor Path) across the leat, and beyond it is a large boulder which apparently proved intractable for the mason who attempted to work it.

At the headweir are the posts of a former sluice, apparently now redundant and similar to those at the original Doe Tor Brook intake, where the water courses naturally from a pool into the banked channel. The remaining, upper reach of the leat fell into disuse when mining ceased at Wheal Jewell. Upstream from the headweir another boulder has been partly worked, this time resulting in a potential trough. A few yards above the headweir is the entry, on the right bank, of the disused portion of the leat, which cascaded over granite in the deep channel extending upward to a sharp northward bend. Note that OS do not show the disused leat; the broken line marked at 589537 is a reave-wall crossing the hillside just below the channel.

An uneventful course takes the walker into the clitter of Doe Tor, where great labour was expended on cutting the channel. A large horizontal slab forms a bridge over the leat where the miners had to clear an earthen channel below the rock to admit the flow.

The channel now curves below Doe Tor to reach the valley floor, where the old sluice-posts are seen at the intake at the foot of a wide pool, and several stones of the deflecting weir still remain in place. Small cataracts occur above the pool, though the more impressive Doe Tor Falls are further downstream; water still enters the old channel and flows for a short way before escaping through the breached bank into the brook.

This wild little valley between Doe Tor and the cross-surmounted Brai Tor (a 13ft (4m) high monument placed there in 1887 by Dartmoor painter William Widgery in honour of Queen Victoria's Golden Jubilee) is beautiful in the extreme, the falls downstream from the leat-head providing a major attraction and an ideal place to take children. In the main Lyd valley, the river emerges from Black Rock Falls under the long sweep of High Down, the entire scene providing a satisfying climax to the easy walk detailed in this chapter.

6
Hamlyn's (Holne Moor) Leat

4½ miles (7.2km)   Map 4

Historical digest
Buckfastleigh was for centuries an important cloth-manufacturing town, and the wool-jobbers' track crossed south Dartmoor from Buckfastleigh to the wool-collecting centre of Sheepstor on the southwest moor; there are, indeed, in places survivals of the industry to the present day. Helen Harris states in *Industrial Archaeology of Dartmoor* that Joseph Hamlyn and his three sons started fellmongering there – buying sheepskins to sell the wool and pelts separately – in 1806. They later acquired fresh premises and, at the end of the century, the Hamlyn family were leaders in the Buckfastleigh woollen industry. They had also bought the ancient Buckfastleigh Higher Mill and needed a satisfactory head of water for power; the neighbouring Holy Brook was hardly equal to the task, even in normal flow, and the problem was solved by leating water from a reliable source on the high moor to supplement the volume of the brook, then at a point lower downstream extracting the needed flow for the woollen-mill waterwheel. O Brook on Holne Moor was selected as the source and Holy Brook at Michelcombe the terminal; hence we read 'Holne Moor leat' on maps but on the Moor hear only of 'Hamlyn's Leat'.

In 1953 Higher Buckfast Mill was purchased and adapted to their particular processes by the Buckfastleigh Plating Company Ltd. To this day Hamlyn's leat performs its original function of supplementing the volume of Holy Brook to supply the lower leat to the mill; the water is taken in at Hockmoor Plantation and flows through a long, high wooden launder to enter the mill, where its supply is used for rinsing purposes.

The leat throughout most of its moorland course flows very near (and parallel with) the old Wheal Emma channel; the reader is therefore requested to refer to information on both channels on pp87–95 of Walk 10. The greater part of Holne Moor is so heavily scored by reaves, leats flowing and disused, and tinners' water channels and tracks, that distant views from the north area (of Holne Moor) are common to both leats.

Following the moorland leat (DOWN)
Drive to Cumston Tor car park (670718) and walk southwestward down the slope of Horn's Hill to the intake of the leat at 663712. A simple little stone weir extends from a boulder under the brook's left bank and deflects water into the channel. Downstream are a flood-relief channel and a wide pool, and beyond them a picturesque, small clapper bridge placed obliquely over the leat; this carries a path that crosses both the Wheal Emma channel (see p91) and the disused Cumston leat, above. All three leats remain in close mutual proximity for some distance. Cumston Farm sits on the hillside below and the great bulk of Holne Moor is prominent above, right. As the leat curves eastward on the spur of the hill, a branch channel descends to Cumston Farm. That this was originally a part of the Cumston leat before the Hamlyn's channel was cut is clear from its direct alignment with the dry portion. The Cumston leat now disappears from the scene and the stones of a prehistoric field system trace geometrical patterns on the hillside between the two remaining channels; there are bridges carrying paths to those on the higher, Wheal Emma leat. On the brink of the Aller Brook valley, Hamlyn's leat is piped across, the channel rounding the next hill-spur and giving fine views (see p93).

Reaching the Holne road, the flow of the leat enters an underground pipe; this passes across the Venford valley beneath the dam roadway to emerge, entirely by gravity, at a point only 16ft (5m) lower, on the side of Rickett's Hill. The dry channel, meanwhile, continues above the reservoir and crosses three gerts watered by branches of Venford Brook, its contour-looping in general less acute than that of the Wheal Emma above (see p94). Constructional skill is shown in the banked S-bend above Venford Bottom, from where the dry channel again reaches the Holne road, this time a little above the point where the broad, green way of the pre-reservoir road leaves it to approach its former crossing of Venford Brook (on a now submerged arch-bridge). North of the road the channel regains its flow of (piped) water on the 1,015ft (310m) contour;

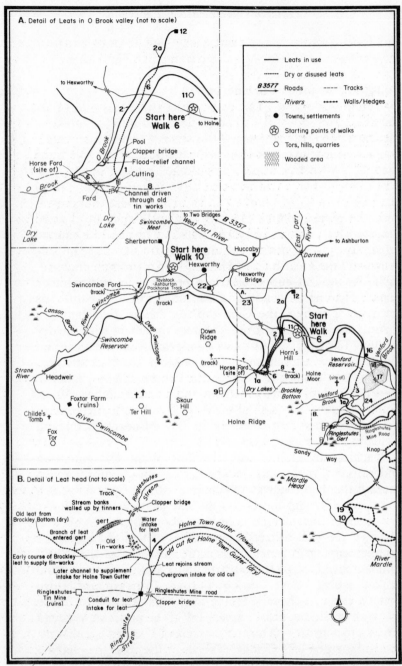

Map 4 showing Walk 6 Hamlyn's (Holne Moor) Leat; Walk 7 Holne Town Gutter; Walk 10 Wheal Emma Leat, with detail of Leats in O Brook Valley and Leat head

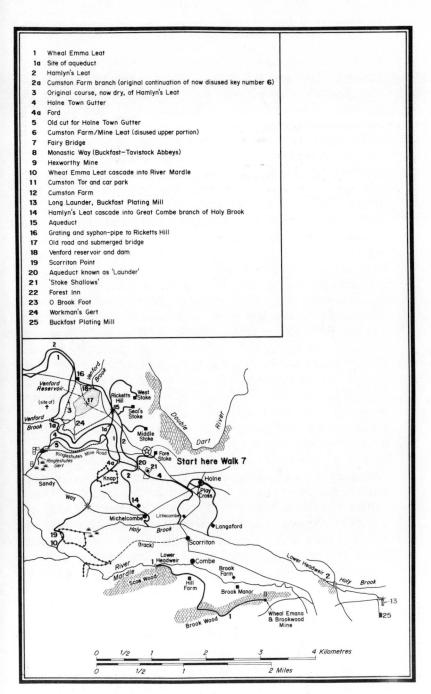

this flows through a wide-mouthed pipe (resembling the bell of a bass-euphonium) into a small concrete chamber, from where the original channel now carries the water beneath the aqueducted Stoke Farm leat. Then follows a hairpin bend to reach and pass below the Holne road for the fourth time, on the east brow of the hill. Flowing well below the spur of Holne Lee, it passes beneath a clapper cart-bridge carrying the Ringleshutes mine road. Crossing the plain of Sholedon near the Stoke enclosures and supplying branches to the Stoke farms, one branch leaving it near the Holne road to serve Fore Stoke, it is forded near the wall-surrounded house named 'Stoke Shallows' (formerly 'The Shanty') by a moorland track on the line of the Buckfast-Tavistock monastic way (ascending from the former Sholedon moorgate). Now curving westward to reach Great Combe, it is carried over the Holne Town gutter on a wooden aqueduct, the place being locally known as 'Launder'. A wooden sluice once moved between vertical granite slabs, its purpose explained on p67. A short way westward the leat again bends sharply (to the south) to enter Great Combe, where its water flows to a confluence with Holy Brook. During the arctic February of 1985, the usual headlong rush of the leat was transformed into a frozen icicle-bedecked waterfall. The view from here towards the bold hills of Pupers and Snowdon, embracing the transition between high moor and border-country, is very pleasing.

The intake from Holy Brook for the lower leat is a considerable way downstream. The brook passes through Michel Combe, beneath Langaford Bridge (south of Holne village), between Burchetts Wood and Hembury Woods and enters Hockmoor Plantation; here, at the northwest tip of the wood at 728678, is the small headweir and an iron sluice-gate, its control-wheel padlocked to prevent interference. A liberal flow enters the leat, which passes along the lower edge of the wood just above the brook.

Following the lower leat (DOWN)

Take the Buckfast-Hembury road to Hembury Bridge (731677). Park; return up the road to where it crosses the leat. Pass through a wooden gate (right) and follow the permitted path (not a right of way), which at first curves slightly away from the leat before descending to the headweir. The pastoral view through the trees of the steeply wooded, opposite valley-side epitomises the Dartmoor border-country in this locality. East of the road the leat passes through farm fields at the rear of private gardens, before bending to enter that of 'Sideham'. Here it is visible from the north roadside bridge parapet (at 739675) entering a pond, below which some masonry is the sole relic of the former float-valve control that maintained a steady flow of water from the pond into the mill launder; the latter, leading to the site of the former woollen-mill waterwheel, may be seen from the side of the shop on the south roadside.

The grounds of the mill may not be entered for reasons of security connected with its present manufacturing processes, for which a constant supply of clean water is needed for rinsing purposes. It is perhaps to be regretted that the regular maintenance once carried out over the entire course of the leat by the Hamlyn management, when a large waterwheel had to be powered, is now discontinued, as the plating company finds the volume of Holy Brook alone to be adequate to their need. The Stoke farm branches, however, and the facility at Launder for supplementing the Holne village supply, ensures that enough periodical work will be done by other interested parties to maintain the continued life of this interesting leat.

7
Holne Town Gutter

3¾ miles (6km)   Map 4

Historical digest
The course of this leat – 'gutter' being the word in general use on
Dartmoor for a water channel of any sort – demonstrated its
seniority over the Wheal Emma and Hamlyn's leats by obliging
the builders thereof to avoid interference with its course. The
'gutter' is accompanied for some way by an even older channel
which, long disused, was taken in from the stream in
Ringleshutes Gert above the headweir of the gutter and once
delivered water to the Stoke farms. Its moorland course is also
described in this chapter from the north foot of Holne Lee to its
source in the gert.

A singular attraction of the Holne Town gutter is the
impression of height received at the headweir: the central basin
is spread out below the observer like a map placed on the floor –
an impression abiding throughout the moorland course of this
elevated channel.

The leat has a great number of delivery points, branches
being visible to the walker – in some places even to the motorist –
on roadsides near Play Cross, Vicarage Cross, the village centre
and in the new burial ground of the parish church. The several
leat 'tails' unite below the village and descend steeply to join
Holy Brook at Langaford. Of these points, the most interesting
is the village centre, through which the leat comes leaping down
past the Post Office, Church House Inn, and Holne Court.

Following the leat (UP)
Drive to Holne Moorgate (cattle-grid) and park in the disused
roadside quarry at 698699. Follow the track along the boundary
wall of the enclosures (left); at Stoke Shallows (see p64) turn
uphill and continue to follow the estate wall as it bends (left)
downhill from its higher corner. The leat is here seen entering
the west wall through a small, arched portal; below the estate it
passes over a lane and stream (**no access**) into farm fields to
distribute its branches.

66

Walk upstream. Flowing on the plain of Sholedon, the leat passes below a wooden aqueduct at 'Launder' (see p64) carrying Hamlyn's leat. The large sluice seen here was, by agreement with the Hamlyn management, operated to admit water on one day in each year into the gutter; branches of the latter were also closed to augment the head of water, which then turned a waterwheel at Holne Court for driving threshing machinery. The unweathered appearance of the sluice is due to its renewal by the Dartmoor National Park Authority in April 1985. From Launder, the leat makes directly for the Wheal Emma (dry) channel. Here no aqueduct was required on the level plain and the junction of the waters was controlled as needed by agreement and by the manipulation of stones; at this point a track between Holne Moorgate and the Sandy Way forded the confluence – the OS marking 'Ford' being correct – though, of course, only one leat is now flowing.

Follow the channel bending northward and passing a clapper cart-bridge carrying the Ringleshutes mine road. In a short distance it reaches its loop on the north spur of Holne Lee, which is bisected by the twin lines of a reave and an accompanying track which passes within a few yards of a Paignton Urban District Council stone and a ruined Bronze Age cairn within the loop; the track is the Buckfast-Tavistock monastic way, which descends the hill northwestward beyond the leat to Venford Bottom.

At the head of the loop a bull's-eye stone and grating control a branch channel to West Stoke Farm below; fifty paces downstream from this point the old cut joins the flowing channel which from then on is, of course, the original. Examine the bend in the dry channel (near the bull's-eye); despite being overgrown through long disuse, it is well defined here and throughout its course. It is the higher of the two channels and when following it the walker will have the gutter almost within arm's reach a few yards to his right.

Continue westward between the two channels; notice a converging track, left; this wide, stony way is the Ringleshutes mine road and the three lines remain in close proximity as they cross a small plain at the shallow head of a tinners' gert, right; the depth of this, Workman's Gert, greatly increases as it drops directly to the head of the reservoir in Venford Bottom. A reave runs (just below and parallel with the Holne gutter) from the head of the gert to that next westward – Ringleshutes Gert: it appears to have been the upper boundary of an area of prehistoric land-allocation. This is an altogether pleasant place to walk, good ground, lofty and commanding good views over a part of the central basin to the eastern highlands of the Moor, also the monastic way beyond Brockley Bottom – furthest of the Venford headwater valleys – can be detected climbing from Venford Bottom to the site of Two Thorns Cross and continuing to Horn's Cross on Horn's Hill. Both leats take a sinuous course across the plain, where a few thorn trees struggle to survive winter's harsh northeast winds near a PUDC stone. The courses of no less than four leats on Holne Moor can be seen from here: the present two channels, flowing and disused, the Wheal Emma, and Hamlyn's leat crossing the Holne road far below. The reservoir scene was unusually enhanced, during field work for this chapter in February 1985, by ice-coated water and by frozen snow adorning the surrounding trees.

On the spur of the hill between the mine road and the ancient leat is an old mining pit in which stands a set stone; uninscribed, its firm setting shows that it once had particular significance, perhaps as a mining boundary mark. The twin leats now approach their headweirs in Ringleshutes Gert. This large, artificially deepened valley contains relics of the old mine from which the gert took its name; these include the mine-house, the base of a collapsed chimney stack and the pit for the wheel that provided power for ore-crushing stamps. Despite the great labour inevitably involved in raising and processing ore, operations at the mine were short-lived and consisted only of surface workings: no records of output are known. From the remains of the mine, the road runs up the valley to join the Sandy Way and climbs to the head of Ringleshutes Gert, where it is intersected by the old Cumston-Dockwell track passing towards Hapstead Ford on the River Mardle. Fig B (p62) is intended to help the reader interpret the complicated leating system in Ringleshutes Gert.

8
Gidleigh Leat

4½ miles (7.2km)   Map 5

Historical digest

This channel could appropriately have been known as the
'Gidleigh Town Gutter', its function being similar to that of the
Holne Town Gutter, with the addition of watering a drift pound
recorded in antiquity. Like the Holne leat, its source lies in a
striking scenic setting with, in this case, views across the
magnificent middle-reach basin of the North Teign river.
Branches and delivery points are numerous, the channels
threading a practically unspoilt piece of Dartmoor border-
country before the water finally reaches Blackaton Brook below
Gidleighmill Farm. In former years, eight farmers in the
parish, including moorman Will Jordan of Moortown, each
undertook to carry out one day of maintenance on the leat
annually; this, as in other places, has now declined to
haphazard work to keep the leat flowing. Times have changed.

Following the leat (DOWN)

Drive to Berrydown Gate (662877). The best approaches are
from Chagford via Gidleigh, or along the A30 road from
Okehampton. In the latter case, branch right at 649932;
continue past Shilstone, Great Ensworthy and Moortown; fork
right via Glebe Farm to Berrydown, but turn right at the
T-junction to reach Berrydown Gate (and not left to Berrydown
Farm). There is ample parking space opposite the entrance to
Scorhill House; the stream flowing beneath the moorgate here
is the leat.

Walk through the gateway, cross the leat-ford and follow the
wide funnel of Berrydown Stroll; notice the water, a rushing
stream emerging from the Scorhill enclosures, left, and a fine
sheep-creep in an enclosure wall, right. Follow the track
leading northwest between the rounded Scorhill (left) and
Butter Hill (right). Notice the large surrounding area where
'vags' (thin slabs of surface peat) have been cut over the

69

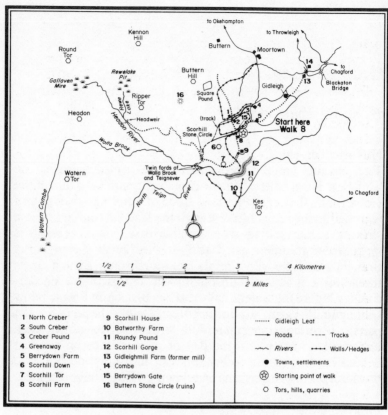

Map 5 showing Walk 8 Gidleigh Leat

1	North Creber	9	Scorhill House
2	South Creber	10	Batworthy Farm
3	Creber Pound	11	Roundy Pound
4	Greenaway	12	Scorhill Gorge
5	Berrydown Farm	13	Gidleighmill Farm (former mill)
6	Scorhill Down	14	Combe
7	Scorhill Tor	15	Berrydown Gate
8	Scorhill Farm	16	Buttern Stone Circle (ruins)

······· Gidleigh Leat

⟶ Roads ---- Tracks

〰 *Rivers* ••••• Walls/Hedges

● Towns, settlements

✪ Starting point of walk

○ Tors, hills, quarries

Map 5 showing Walk 8 Gidleigh Leat

centuries. Walk towards the (also rounded) Ripper Tor, but make a wide sweep (right) to avoid the miry plain under the east slope of the tor; this will enable the walker to take in the ruined (unrestored) Buttern stone circle (659884), of which only a few stones are now standing. The low rocks on the hilltop above the monument are Buttern Rocks. On approaching Ripper Tor, be certain to cross the upper ends of two rocky hollows. Reaching the little tor – a small island amid a sea of huge, billowing hills – pause to survey the splendid view over the Teign basin and its enclosing heights. Notable features are (left to right) the sinuous, silver leat approaching Scorhill, Kes Tor, the long sweep of Shoveldon, the afforested Lang Ridge, Siddaford Tor above the North Teign valley and the prow of Hangingstone Hill etching a bold skyline between Watern and Wild Tors at

70

nearly 2,000ft (610m). The south slope of Ripper Tor is marked by rock-streams, the ice-transported debris of the tor during its siege by the extreme frosts and snowfalls of the last Ice Age.

Walk southwest towards Watern Tor – a lofty and striking series of piles on Watern Down which includes the Thurlestone, or holed rock – and descend to the beautiful, hidden combe watered by the Headon river: the OS versions 'Gallaven Brook' and (upstream) 'Gartaven Ford' are never used, and Headon River is a sub-tributary of the North Teign via Walla Brook. Beyond the valley rises the down from which the stream is named, Headon or Heydon – the 'high down'; it is highest of the minor heights below Watern Tor and appears as 'Hey Down' in a Duchy of Cornwall document of 13 May 1803. As the walker descends the hillside the lower reach of the stream, where the leat is taken in opposite a re-entrant in the west valley-side, will become visible.

A considerable volume of water reaches the headweir; not only is Gallaven (not 'Gartaven') Mire, source of Headon River quite extensive, but the river's first and only tributary Rewe Lake (OS 'Ruelake') comes from its own deep mire in Rewelake Pit at the head of the tin workings known as Whitey Works, and falls into the major stream from a hanging mire. Another tributary source, now dry, was the leat from Willtor Well. This was cut to further supplement volume for the headweir, in order to compensate for the branch channel to the mine workings at Bradmere (OS 'Bradford') Pool (see p74). The leat received its supply at the head of Willtor Well – a huge and copious spring under Wild Tor – crossed the shallow re-entrant between the Wild Tor ridge and Headon and contoured the latter high above the Walla Brook valley floor to deliver its burden from Headon River. Control of the leat supply might be described as automatic; the weir is arranged to admit a large percentage of the river's flow, and as it rounds the south foot of Ripper Tor an overflow channel returns surplus water to the river below. The combe is enhanced by cascades, rowan and willow trees and opens towards the dominating Kes Tor; on the valley floor above the headweir are two unusual tinners' caches, one of oblong shape and obviously intended for the concealment of tools.

The walker is warned that to follow the actual course of the leat will involve him in some unpleasantly wet, spongy walking; even in dry weather he will encounter an unwelcome mixture of miry ground, tussocks and dwarf-gorse. It is therefore advisable to leave the leat when it nears the bad ground and walk northward at the east foot of Ripper Tor; recross the re-entrant (right) at the head of the two rocky hollows (see p70) and join a well defined track, the Sandy Road, which comes out from Berrydown and Creber Strolls to Gallaven Ford on Headon River. This excellent track keeps well above the marshy plain threaded by the leat, though it does not go as far north as Buttern Circle and therefore makes an ideal return route to Berrydown. To return to the channel, leave the track beyond a streamlet at Sandy Ford and follow the sunken way to the Buttern-Scorhill saddle. The monumental Scorhill circle will now be visible backed by Batworthy plantation, the leat passing beside it. Return to the leat by crossing a clear, grassy patch to where it emerges from the marshy ground and forms a wide pool beside a large, flat rock on the left bank.

Walk downstream from the pool and observe that (at least) three monoliths, removed long ago for the purpose from Scorhill circle, have been used in banking the leat (Pl. 8). The converging streams of North Teign and Walla Brook crossing the twin fords at Teignever are now seen, and the leat flows beneath a clapper cart-bridge carrying the track from Creber to

Plate 8   Gidleigh Leat near Scorhill Circle: Notice stones removed from the circle for banking the lower side of the leat. In the distance are Teignhead, Great Newtake, Woodhole Pit and Wood Lake (os 'Hew' Lake)

Teignever, which bisects the stone circle. Next walk up to the circle, a very fine monument 88ft (27m) in diameter with 23 stones erect and 7 fallen. Return along the track to the leat; follow it along the flank of Scorhill Down to the rockpile ahead. Scorhill Tor commands a view of romantic beauty; beneath it (and the leat) are the woodlands of Scorhill Gorge and beyond them the hut-homes and field enclosures of Iron Age man on Teigncombe Common, overlooked by the block-like Kes Tor. Much stone-cutting is in evidence around the tor which now consists of a small remnant tor amidst a clitter of slabs, and near the leat is a hut circle with a diameter of 29ft (9m) – perhaps of the middle or late Bronze Age – certainly pre-dating the far larger hutted homes on Teigncombe Common.

Curving with the hill, the leat now enters the enclosures of Scorhill House beneath a bridging stone in the massive, nineteenth-century boundary wall. (The reader must now follow this northwestward to Berrydown Stroll .) Within the grounds the leat passes through the garden of Scorhill Lodge and through a wall-aperture in Berrydown Stroll (see p69). Before leaving the stroll the leat branches, right, to Berrydown Cottage and Farm, approaching which it is seen in a gutter beside the road from Berrydown Gate to Gidleigh village, and left to the Creber (OS 'Creaber') farms and the old drift pound.

To deal first with the left branch. Walk from the head of Berrydown Stroll outside the enclosure wall to that of Creber Stroll. Descend to the moorgate and the old settlement. Notice the deserted, small longhouse of North Creber, left, last occupied by a member of the Endacott family; opposite this, right, look over a field gate and observe the leat approaching from Berrydown Stroll. It enters the hamlet below a bridging stone, is joined by a streamlet flowing through Creber Stroll, extends a diminutive branch to the deserted farm and another to South Creber, passes through an iron conduit beneath the road and flows alongside its north verge to supply Creber Pound. I have described this in *High Dartmoor* as having

> lost the gates that made impounding possible. The visitor may spare himself the search for a traditional pound, for here it is no more than a small, diamond-shaped common between the farms, its sides enclosed and ends controlled by gates. The posts of the lower, known as 'Tipson Gate', still remain; the higher gateway, too

narrow for a modern tractor, surrendered its posts some years ago
. . . Creber Pound has not been used for fifty years, but many of the
senior moormen of Teign country can well remember it teeming
with bullocks or ponies – have, indeed, helped to drive them there.

One of those moormen is Will Jordan of Moortown, who
recalled for me that, on drift days, the landlord of the George
Inn in Okehampton was paid by the Duchy to prepare and
deliver refreshments to the moormen drifters at the pound.

From Creber Pound, the water served Greenaway and other
farms and fields. I am informed by Will Jordan that a branch
channel crossed the South Creber fields, contour-looped the
valleys of Moortown Brook and Forder Brook and, there
augmenting its flow, traversed the east flank of Buttern Hill
below Square Pound (which was used by the local moormen
when gathering herds from the in-country for summertime
moorland grazing) and over Clannaborough Down to reach
Blackaton Brook at Shilla Pool; here it was aqueducted across
the valley and descended to the in-country via Week and
Gooseford to supply the old tin-works at Bradmere (OS
'Bradford') Pool near Spinsters Rock. A portion of this leat
follows (approximately) the 1,150ft (350m) contour across
Clannaborough Down and passes through an Iron Age
settlement.

To see the arrival of the Berrydown Farm branch-leat in the
village centre, drive to Gidleigh and park near the church. Walk
through the churchyard to the upper wall and observe the leat
approaching through the Berrydown fields and passing through
a small paddock at the rear of the Youth Hostel. Entering
beneath a bridging stone, it flows across the churchyard at the
east end of the church and passes beneath another such stone to
the roadside, where it passes beneath the road to flow alongside
the south wall of the (formerly unenclosed) village green and
enter a field gateway opposite some cottages. There is no space
here to describe the rural bliss of Gidleigh, with ancient church
and Norman fortified manor house, but the walker is well
advised to allow himself time to absorb it.

The leat descends from the gateway, from where a public
path once ran to Gidleigh Mill, now Gidleighmill Farm (Mr
Ernie Bowden). The establishing of a mill here is thought to
pre-date the building in *c*1142 of the manor – or Gidleigh Castle,

as it is usually known. From the mill-pool and waterwheel (the latter long vanished) the water joined Moortown Brook, which itself flows into Forder Brook before entering Blackaton Brook at Blackaton Bridge. Unless the reader plans to walk through the fascinating labyrinth of border-country lanes between Gidleigh and Chagford, he is advised to drive north from Gidleigh village to the road junction at 672891 and there turn right; continue past Coombe and Gidleighmill Farm to Blackaton Bridge. If he is to enjoy the unique and rugged attractions of this historic and remote piece of Dartmoor borderland, he will need a car of modest dimension and a natural facility for reversing it!

9
Plymouth, or Drake's, Leat

6¾ miles (10.9km)   Map 1

Historical digest

The growing mercantile importance of Plymouth in the late sixteenth century resulted in increasing demands for a reliable supply of fresh water, for which the existing springs and conduits then tapped had become totally inadequate. An Act was passed by Parliament in 1585 (27 Elizabeth I) authorising the City Corporation to 'digge a Trenche throughe and over all the landes and groundes lying between Plymouth and anye parts of the said river of Mew'. The celebrated Sir Francis Drake, already nationally famous, was appointed to carry out the task for a fee of £300, out of which he had to finance the work and pay compensation to the landowners affected. Robert Lampan of St Budeaux (now a part of Plymouth) was the capable surveyor, local tinners were employed to cut the entire channel and Drake cut the first sod in December 1590. The leat, from 6ft to 7ft (1.8 to 2.1m) wide and 18½ miles (29.8km) long, was completed on 23 April 1591. 'No provision was made in the Act for compensation water, and the whole flow of the stream was taken when required. There were times, of course, when the inhabitants suffered serious inconvenience through frost and snow, and in flood times, through dirty water' (*The Plymouth Water Undertaking*, Frank Howarth, 1934).

Water was to be leated from the middle moorland reach of the River Mewy or Mew (OS 'Meavy'), where a wide headweir and sluice were constructed just below Lower Lowery – an abandoned farm of which a barn still remains above water level. The leat followed the river's right bank, its course below Burrator dam being marked by a green, valley-side level, where description begins.

It is interesting to reflect that the sixteenth- and seventeenth-century millers of Meavy village mill would, in a dry season when the leat drew a capacity load from the river, have had to rely for their head of water upon the incoming waters of

Sheepstor Brook augmented by any overflow from the leat between Headweir and the mill.

Mrs Eliza Bray, in volume 2 of her *A Description of the Part of Devonshire bordering on the Tamar and the Tavy*, gives a legendary account of Drake's speed and efficiency in bringing the water into Plymouth:

> The people of Plymouth were so destitute of water in the reign of Queen Elizabeth, that they were obliged to send their clothes to Plympton to be washed in fresh water. Sir Francis Drake resolved to rid them of this inconvenience. So he called for his horse, mounted, rode to Dartmoor, and hunted about till he found a very fine spring. Having fixed on one that would suit his purpose, he gave a smart lash to his horse's side, pronouncing as he did so some magical words, when off went the animal as fast as he could gallop, and the stream followed his heels all the way into the town. This assuredly was not only the most wonderful, but the most cheap and expeditious mode of forming a canal ever known or recorded by tradition.

There are still places within the city limits where the leat may be glimpsed piecemeal, but they cannot all be identified and described here; some are shown on the 1935 edition of the OS six-inch map. The longest continuous portion borders the Crownhill waterworks grounds, where it lies near the Devonport leat and, like that channel, for a short way follows the moat of Crownhill Fort; here, for a reason not now known, a short tunnel was driven to connect the leats.

There is public access to Drake's Place on North Hill, where roadside parking is normally possible. Enter the gardens below the reservoir west of the road and notice a short open conduit passing from below the reservoir wall to Sherwell United Reformed Church; this was once the water supply to the waterwheel of Sherwell corn mill, its site now occupied by the church. The 'waste leat' then crossed Union Street and supplied other mills – including tucking, canvas, tanning and cement works – in Mill Street, Russell Street and Mill Bay, from which the waste water flowed into the bay. Next examine the roadside conduit and trough; inserted in the wall above is a stone bearing the inscription, 'Made in the maioraltie of John Trelawnie 1598'; another inscription reads, '1834 – Removed from Old Town Street'. The building of distribution conduits for the water had begun in 1592 and twenty-seven were made in all.

It is remarkable that the leat carried its burden of fresh water to the growing city for over 300 years. In 1871 the channel was given a lining of granite slabs, although some were unlawfully removed during the early years of this century for use elsewhere. According to my observations, stones number on average 175 per side in 100yd (91m); the consequent labour of this task is therefore calculable only in staggering figures: at 6,160 slabs to the mile (1.6km), 113,950 would have been quarried, cut, shaped, transported and positioned. The P&DR (tramroad) had by this time fallen into disuse, and the GWR's Yelverton-Princetown branch lay twelve years ahead; but probably the tramroad was put in working order for the transportation of the stones from the Walkham quarries to within easy reach of the leat throughout its moorland course as far as the southern end of Roborough Down, where the divergence between tramroad and leat was one both of elevation and geographical distance. Twenty-seven years later this entire undertaking became redundant upon the opening of the new reservoir at Burrator and a piped water supply to the city's reservoirs.

Following the leat (DOWN)
Drive to Burrator dam; park; enter the roadside gate and descend to the valley-side shelf (Pl. 9). Turn left and walk to the wall of the dam. At this point the gorge closes in and Drake's problems began; to conduct the leat along the rocky valley-side he utilised long wooden conduits – in the words of a contemporary account – for '448 paces through mightie rockes which was thought impossible to carrie water through'. There is, of course, no remaining sign of the conduits, but the rearing wall of the modern dam is impressive from below. A huge clitter streams from the gorge-side and Ringmoor Down is visible through the trees, whilst above the opposite valley-side is the rounded, wooded hill from which the tree-concealed Berra Tor outcrops. The tor rocks are worth a visit, and are reached easily by crossing the dam and the stile beyond into the woodlands, right. The tor provides the origin of the locality name, Burrator, the etymology being 'Beara Tor' (the tor in the *beare*,

78

Plate 9   SPENCER MAP *annotated by John Spencer, showing courses of Devonport and Plymouth Leats in Mewy Valley:* Notice the carefully marked course of the pre-reservoir River Mewy (OS 'Meavy'). The leat shown crossing the south flank of Sheeps Tor is the still flowing Longstone Leat

or wood) = Berra Tor = Burrator.

From the dam follow the level, grassy way, actually an infilled portion of the leat; the channel first opens to the vision 100yd (91m) before reaching the wide concrete bridge carrying a track from the road above. Continue along the left bank below the huge crag of Claig Tor, or Yannadon Crag, which looms above the trees, right. Gradually the steep, wooded slope opposite recedes, the sound of Sheepstor Brook falling to the river is heard, and Lynch Down appears through the trees. This is altogether a very beautiful woodland walk, but do not follow the Dartmoor National Park yellow dots now appearing, for they lead towards the riverside path to Meavy village.

When virtually at the end of Burrator Gorge, notice the smooth outline of Yannadon Down above the thinning woodland, right, and a 'PCWW 1917' post (marking the Plymouth Corporation Water Works ownership of the Plymouth leat at that time) at the beginning of a left-bank leatside wall. Follow the path along the top of the (wide) wall, which was built to buttress the granite-lined channel against collapse onto the steep hillside below. Eventually the wall ceases and Meavy village comes into view, whilst Catstor and Ringmoor Downs rise, left, above the valley woodlands. Pass a clapper footbridge, where the easiest walking is along the bed of the leat, which is stepped in places to reduce erosion by the rapid current. Soon the trees come to an end and an extensive view opens across the Mewy valley from Wigford Down to Yelverton. A fine clapper cart-bridge of seven imposts links the farmlands below with the open moor of Yannadon, where the line of the old GWR Princetown branch is seen rounding the flank. The bridge next ahead, clapper-based, carries the Dousland-Meavy road (an ancient way once used by monks travelling between Plympton Priory and Tavistock Abbey).

Beyond the bridge, a succession of farm fields and building developments intervene before the next (and final) passage of unrestricted access across the open moorland of Roborough Down. Through the kindness of Mr W. Vanstone of Meavy Barton, readers may climb the south roadside leat-bridge parapet into field 1 and follow the leat bank to the next bridge, which carries the narrow South Lake Lane. A fine set of wall-steps leads into the lane, and another set, overgrown, is seen on the opposite side. Mount to the lane and follow it to the left; **do not enter the private ground opposite.** Notice that the owner of a lane-side house has succeeded in rescuing from oblivion a former GWR level-crossing gate to head his drive. Beyond it is a farmyard gate labelled 'South Lake Farm', beyond which the leat channel is visible, right. **Do not enter:** a description of this portion of the leat now follows, but the walker must view the further end of it from Lake Lane (see below).

Field 1: the channel is spanned by a cart-bridge. Two troughs are neatly inserted in the hedge bordering the leat to receive overflow water; this was made possible by the high level of the channel above the field, the hedge having been substantially reinforced and 'bound' by a planted hedgerow. *Field 2*: a similar trough has been inserted in the hedge. A strong optical illusion occurs here – one common on Dartmoor leats – of the water flowing *up*hill in downstream direction; something impossible, of course, in a gravitational channel. The view of the Mewy valley is delightful from here. The further gate opens upon an ancient, transverse lane, where restricted width and high hedges show its origin as a packhorse way; it crosses the leat on a now largely overgrown clapper bridge. *Field 3*: another leat-filled trough appears in the hedge. *Field 4*: as for field 3; the field is bounded by Lake Lane, where the leat passes beneath a bridge beside the house named 'Moorcroft'. The overgrown channel can be seen continuing from the bridge below the garden of the house.

Next, drive towards Dousland; opposite a post-box (right), turn left into Lake Lane and view the leat leaving field 4 and passing below the garden of Moorcroft. Drive along the lane beyond a hollow, to the hill ahead; stop at the next bridge and park tightly into the gateway, left. Before continuing the walk, call personally at Cowards Lake Farm caravan and ask permission of Mr or Mrs A. Cole to follow the channel through their fields south of the lane to Westella Road, Yelverton. Mr T. W. Eggins, owner of the two fields north of the lane (fields 5 and 6), is kindly willing for walkers *without dogs* to enter the laneside gateway and inspect the channel. From the leat bridge, therefore, proceed as follows: enter field 5 (right); walk upstream along the right bank. Notice some drilled granite blocks in the banking of the leat – sets removed from the nearby

P&DR. The GWR line and B3212 are to the walker's left beyond a bus garage; a clapper bridge appears, and the contour-loop of the leat between here and Moorcroft can be seen. There is open entry to field 6; beyond it is a private garden where the leat channel has been converted into an ornamental pond. **Go no further**, but return to Lake Lane bridge.

Now enter (**with no dog**) the fields of Cowards Lake Farm south of the bridge. *Field 1*: notice a clapper in mid-field and the well-controlled curve of the leat. *Field 2*: the GWR embankment overshadows the leat, and the Devonport channel appears unexpectedly on the scene to run parallel with the Plymouth. When the railway bears away right, the twin channels pass beneath twin bridges (Pl. 10). *Field 3*: another pair of bridges and a delightful view (left to right) of Peak Hill, Yannadon, Sheeps and Gutter Tors and Ringmoor Down, backed by the lofty Plym ridge and Shiel Top. (The Devonport now becomes overgrown: see p16). Enter *field 4*: the Plymouth leat remains clear in running towards the houses in Westella Road; both leats were aqueducted across the railway cutting (now infilled) beyond which they flowed beneath road bridges and passed behind private gardens to reach two bridges on the south leg of the U-shaped Westella Road.

Plate 10   The Twin Leats, Devonport and Plymouth, in the fields of Cowards Lake Farm: The bridges are (left and concealed by nettles) Devonport Leat and (right) Plymouth Leat. The continuing channels are seen beneath the pine trees. The scene is detailed in the text as field 2

The Plymouth channel may be seen from the bridge parapets including the parapet in Meavy Lane which it approaches as an overgrown ditch, then it passes between St Paul's Church and the vicarage, beneath the vicarage drive beside the church hall and under the bridge in Station Road. This entire portion of the leat may be viewed from the grounds of St Paul's. From Station Road leat bridge, the channel passes through the grounds of 'Woodcroft'. It is advisable to leave a vehicle in the church car park (near Yelverton roundabout); cross Station Road; follow the green way between the wall, left, and the (private) slip-road from the highway, right, to Woodcroft. There are numerous houses here overlooking the Mewy valley, the entrance to each bridged over the leat channel. The lengthy strip of green no-man's land south of Yelverton, usually referred to as 'the Chubbtor road' and connected with the highway by several slip-roads, contains in parallel the Plymouth leat, the P&DR and the Devonport leat.

When Harrowbeer airfield was built at the beginning of World War II, the problem of drainage for such a large, flat expanse was solved by laying a pipe beneath the highway (now the A386) into the old Devonport channel beside the Chubbtor road (see p15); as the continuing channel was no longer maintained, however, leaves and branches caused the water frequently to overflow, and a further length of pipe was laid to carry the airfield drainage into the Plymouth channel. The system still works and the mouth of the pipe is seen below its head in the Devonport channel. In order to ensure the escape of the water, therefore, the SWWA maintains the Plymouth channel as far as a point on Roborough Down beyond Clearbrook, where it is diverted into a flood-relief channel (see p84). It is due to this that, following a period of heavy rainfall, visitors to Clearbrook passing over the leat bridge claim to have seen Drake's leat flowing again!

The best course for the walker on the Chubbtor road is to follow the tramroad, having on his left the granite-lined channel of the Plymouth leat and right, the grassy ditch of the Devonport. Beyond the tramroad milestone another slip-road from the highway gives direct access to Chubb Tor House. The Devonport here diverges to follow a higher contour on Roborough Down than the Plymouth, which enters the Chubb

Tor fields beyond the last house, Little Chubb Tor. **There is no public access to these fields**, but Major J. D. Parkinson, the owner, has allowed me to follow the leat in order to present a complete record of its course.

An overflow spillway in field 1 provided field-irrigation; a clapper cart-bridge spans the channel both here and in field 2, where the serpentine nature of the channel is both unusual and interesting. The enclosed course of the channel ends in field 3 where, at the south boundary hedge, it passes beneath an animal barrier and enters upon the open common of Roborough Down. Most of this no-access portion can be seen from the tramroad above the fields, which remains as a wide, walled lane. Also from here are beautiful views across the Mewy valley to Sheeps Tor and, over the houses of Clearbrook hamlet below the Chubb Tor fields, to Shiel Top and the Plym ridge.

Leat and tramroad emerge respectively from fields and walled lane and continue in close proximity along the east flank of Roborough Down, where they can be followed with ease. A fine clapper spans the leat, followed shortly by a concrete bridge carrying a once much-used track from Clearbrook to Yelverton. Now, at the lower edge of the Yelverton golf course (and still near the tramroad), the leat passes beneath two footbridges to reach the Clearbrook road (leading to the A386) beside Tyrwhitt's tramroad stables. South of the road is a long contour-loop; the tramroad, by virtue of its nature, did not need to follow this, and so briefly diverges from the leat. An ample car park exists near the leat bridge; cross the bridge and turn right into the Clearbrook-Goodameavy byroad for a short way until a clapper bridge over the leat is seen, right; cross this; walk over the open moor (there is little point in following the entire contour-loop) to another clapper bridge, a well-built one with an approach step on either side. This serves an historic track across the down from Goodameavy Bridge to Buckland, being the old monastic way between Buckland Abbey and Plympton Priory; beside the bridge is the deep branch channel cut to carry the airfield drainage (see p83) from the leat into a gully below the Goodameavy road, and so to the River Mewy. For the easiest walking beyond the clapper bridge, follow the bed of the leat. The granite lining, so far in evidence over the course, is interrupted 200yd (183m) beyond an ugly concrete bridge ahead; appearances suggest that the slabs were removed from this portion, when the leat had become redundant, perhaps for road-making. The generally excellent condition of leat-bed and granite lining is due to restorative work carried out by Plymouth Corporation at the beginning of World War II in order to ensure an emergency watercourse to the city in the event of bomb damage to the main supply from Burrator.

The main Clearbrook road, on the plain of the down, throws off a branch to Bickleigh. This crosses the leat on a fine, modern clapper bridge, with dressed-granite portals; this has a width of 40ft (12.2m) in order to carry an oblique crossing of the P&DR, which from here remains on the lower, east side of the leat. The granite lining recommences 100yd (91m) below the bridge, the tramroad here running along the top of the left bank. Another, quite short, unlined portion occurs, then the lining continues to the foot of the open moor at Combe Park.

Granite slabs have in places fallen inwards and a large clapper cart-bridge spans the channel at the head of a hollow in the down, where views across the border-country to the south-west escarpment of the moor and the Plym ridge are good. Beyond the hollow, notice a stone on the left bank containing two drilled holes, a granite set that has somehow strayed from the nearby tramroad. Above, right, a signpost stands at the junction of the Clearbrook road with the highway, whilst ahead is a stand of Scots pines, indicating Combe Park. Remain in the leat channel to Combe Park bridge (carrying Roborough Down Lane from Bickleigh to Maristow), then climb out of it. Beyond the bridge, the leat, enclosed between wire fences, contours fields of the Roborough farms and cannot be followed. Portions of it are visible in Roborough village (in Leat Close, for example) beyond which modern development has largely concealed the channel. From the farm fields it reaches the old Roborough reservoir near the roadside (opposite the Dartmoor National Park sign) at the top of Roborough Hill; the reservoir occupies the site of Roborough Mill which was built in 1820 by Sir Massey Lopes with a lease of sixty-five years, its waterwheel supplied by a launder from the leat. The channel then passes beneath the highway – the bridge parapets remain – into Roborough Plantation, where for a considerable way it runs in close proximity to the Devonport leat (see p11).

Combe Park bridge marks the end of the leat's passage over open moorland and common land and of continuous description here. Readers who wish to see portions of the channel still surviving within the city limits should refer to the historical section of this chapter, p77.

The foregoing description of the famous Drake's Leat cannot end without reference to the annual celebration, over the past 100 years, of the Traditional Survey of the Waterworks and Fishing Feast. R. N. Worth, father of the late Dartmoor authority R. Hansford Worth and himself a historian of Plymouth, suggests that the Fyshinge Feaste originated during the recordership of Sir Francis Drake II (1669–1717). The author and his wife were privileged to attend the 1985 Feast, being the 400th anniversary of the Parliamentary Act of empowerment, at which the Lord Mayor of Plymouth, the Chairman of South West Water Authority (contributor of the Foreword to this book), the Parliamentary Under Secretary of State in the Department of the Environment and other special guests – followed by we ordinary mortals – drank a toast in water taken from the river at Headweir in two highly prized goblets, 'To the Pious Memory of Sir Francis Drake'. A further toast, 'May the Descendants of Him who Brought Us Water Never Want Wine', was then offered during the sipping of red wine from the goblets. Trout caught in the reservoir – by earlier tradition in the leat at the original Headweir, now under 60ft (18m) of water – formed the main dish of the feast that followed. Fine food, wine, a small ensemble providing light music and short, witty speeches contributed to a day that surely would have delighted the indomitable but highly sociable Sir Francis. A small matter of a Spanish invasion fleet in 1588, with which this amazing and diversely talented Elizabethan admiral dealt with great competence, interrupted leat-building for a while, but less than four years later the pure water of Mewy flowed into the city that was so justly proud of him.

The two goblets used at the Feast are respectively inscribed: 'The guift of Sir John Gayer Alderman of London Ano Domini 1648', and, 'The Gyft of John Whyt of London Haberdasher to the Mayor of Plymouth and his Bretheren forever to drink crosse one to ye other at their feastes or meetinges who died 5th June, 1585'.

10
Wheal Emma Leat

9¼ miles (14.9km)   Map 4

Historical digest
The great attribute of this leat for the walker is the scenic variety it provides. The channel was cut from the upper Swincombe river in 1859 to supplement the volume of the River Mardle, from which water was then extracted to drive the wheels of Wheal Emma copper mine near Buckfastleigh. Towards the end of the nineteenth century the working was combined with Brookwood Mine (718675) to form South Devon United. In *The Metalliferous Mining Region of South-west England*, Dines gives production figures for the years 1861–77 as 21,140 tons of 7 per cent copper, and 247 tones of iron pyrite. Harris gives some relevant background information in *Industrial Archaeology of Dartmoor*:

> Around 30,000 tons of copper ore are known to have been raised here during the second half of the nineteenth century. There were six shafts and a number of wheels worked by water from the River Mardle, supplemented by a supply brought from the River Swincombe along a lengthy, tortuous leat . . . Twelve people were employed here in 1870, when the workings were 130 fathoms deep. There are considerable remains – large tips and ruined walls, a sizeable wheel-pit and shafts.

Three short lengths of the leat are affected by access restrictions: these are at Hexworthy, Great Combe Newtake and Scorriton Point. Aqueducts built to carry the leat across streams are marked on early editions of the OS six-inch map. In flowing from the north tip of the southern fen, the River Swincombe makes a sharp north-eastward bend at Sheepfold Corner to reach West Dart at Swincombe Meet. Immediately above the bend it is joined by the River Strane, its waters already swollen by Nuns Cross Brook, which drains Foxtor Mire. This point was selected as suitable for the intake and the Wheal Emma proprietors chose to build their headweir at 622709, though not before some frustration was experienced;

E. A. Robins, the mine manager, complained to Charles
Barrington, the Duchy of Cornwall steward that 'two parties on
the Duchy property have forbidden the contractors to Make the
Leat' (Duchy Princetown Records, 1859). Objections – which,
as Duchy land was involved came probably from the farmers at
the former Foxtor and Higher Swincombe Farms – were finally
overcome and the task was completed in a relatively short time.

Following the leat (DOWN)
To begin on a cautionary note, in case it should appear from the
map that the short walk from Whiteworks to Sheepfold Corner
might form a good approach, the walker should realise that the
leat commences on the opposite bank and that the river can be
very awkward to cross. It is better to approach the headweir by
parking near the Swincombe reservoir road on Gobbet Plain
(647728) and walking via the reservoir; continue along the
valley floor; observe the leat channel (above, left) converging
with the river's course. When the going becomes rough and
wet, climb the hillside and follow the leat UP to the headweir.
Masonry remaining here includes that of a clapper cart-bridge
and the weir and sluices used to deflect Strane Water and so
capture an effective intake. The channel is stone-banked to
prevent collapse onto the steep hillside below, where the
rockfield obviously created problems for the labourers. The
great expanse of Foxtor Mire lies at eye level, ringed by (left to
right) Fox Tor, Stream Hill, Hand Hill, Eylesburrow
Common, Nuns Cross Hill, Peat Cot Hill and Strane Hill. The
picturesque fall of the river in passing from upper to middle
reach is known as the 'Boiler'; notice an ancient, small-capacity
(dry) leat taken in at the foot of the fall and leading to the
grass-covered outline of a small building near the river, which
may have been a stamping-mill for crushing tin ore. This entire
piece of valley is wild, rocky and scenic. From the headweir,
therefore, now follow the leat DOWN.

Beyond a newtake wall of the old Foxtor Farm, carried across
the leat by a bridging-stone (Pl. 11), both river and leat curve
beyond sight and sound of the Boiler, and the first clapper
bridge on the leat appears. The hillside – and the bed of the leat
itself – now becomes marshy, and the best walking is to be found
on the left bank as far as Down Ridge. A hunting gate is seen in

Plate 11   Bridging Stone – Wheal Emma Leat: part of the Dartmoor central basin lies beyond (right)

the wall near the leat, and an associated clapper bridge. Below appears the small Swincombe reservoir, and beyond it the valley of the incoming Lanson Brook cleaves the opposite hillside. Another clapper follows. A prominent, poised rock appears ahead which, although resembling a logan stone, is immovable; it was adopted by prehistoric man as the base of a reave curving up the hillside here. Further on is a crumbled wall of such age that the leat builders disregarded it and drove the channel through it; it leads to a rock outcrop, from which a later, more expertly built wall provides a continuation. Beyond the next clapper the leat enters an area of prehistoric enclosures and reaves where yet another clapper leads to a gate in the continuing wall (right). An enclosed Bronze Age settlement is now seen below the leat, also a thin slab wedged vertically in a frost-parted boulder, its origin in the last Ice Age. Beyond this, a river terrace develops, Down Ridge rises above, and the next clapper bridge appears. Another wall is carried over the leat by a bridging-stone as the channel curves above a Bronze Age village of some extent to approach the wild and beautiful hollow known as Deep Swincombe. Here, a rushing stream and drainage from the steep hillside might have caused much damage to the contour-loop of the leat had it not been carefully lined with granite slabs. Water from the stream still enters the leat, which thus regains its original function for some way. Viewed through the funnel of the hollow are the enclosures of the old Swincombe farms (now used by Sherberton Farm) and the peaceful scene at Swincombe Ford, where substantial stepping stones and wooden clam ('Fairy Bridge') provide alternative means of crossing the river. The wide ford beside them lies on the ancient Tavistock-Ashburton packhorse track. Beyond a small clapper bridge, a wall crosses both Deep Swincombe and the leat on a firm bridging-stone; another bridging-stone follows and, beyond it, a clapper bridge. Below the leat is a hut circle built originally with double walling, 28½ft (8.7m) in diameter. Further along the right bank, a large rock that impeded the channel was cut – the jumper holes are visible – and removed to the opposite bank. A specially constructed overflow channel leads downhill on the east side of the next wall, with the usual bridging-stone; much skill has been used in placing these stones and rebuilding the walls above them.

The leat now draws near to the clearly defined Tavistock-Ashburton track (left), here approaching the wide stroll, known as 'Moor Tongue', which leads to Hexworthy moorgate. A track, formerly much used by the moormen between Hexworthy and Aune Head, comes up from the moorgate through Moor Tongue to a clapper cart-bridge of seven imposts (one collapsed) over the leat. This crosses Moor Tongue and enters the Hexworthy enclosures beneath a substantial bridging-stone; it is spanned by a cart clapper bridge in field 1, and by a smaller bridge in field 2; another cart clapper occurs in field 3 and the channel becomes gorse-choked; passing through field 4 it shortly reaches the Hexworthy mine road. It becomes important here to make clear where public access exists: **do not enter fields 1–4: enter the mine road only from the open moor above and not by the gate at Slade** (above the Forest Inn); **there is no right of way along the lower portion of the mine road.** At Moor Tongue, therefore, view the leat in field 1 from the gate; then follow the outer wall along the flank of Down Ridge, and view the leat in places as it passes through fields 2–4 and crosses the mine road; here it passes obliquely beneath a grassed-over cart clapper bridge 14yd (12.8m) in width.

Descend to the leat (southeast of the mine road) from the outer gate and view it passing through two old enclosures; again, there is **no right of way** through these old newtakes which contain prehistoric reaves and enclosures, and discretion should be used. Two more bridges occur before the leat curves southward to enter the O Brook valley; follow it from where it emerges from the enclosures; miry patches occur and water lies in pools in the leat after heavy rainfall. The sound of West Dart passing through Huccaby Cleave below is loud and clear; after another clapper bridge and an overflow channel, the leat contours a shallow re-entrant, intersects an ancient cornditch and reaches the O Brook valley floor. The three conspicuous parallel lines seen on Horn's Hill, opposite, and on the spur of Cumston Tor, are the Wheal Emma leat (top), the old Cumston leat, and the Holne Moor (Hamlyn's) leat (bottom). Making an acute bend under the rocky hillside, the leat was formerly aqueducted across the valley – as well as taking in water from O Brook. All signs of this piece of water engineering and Horse Ford downstream were swept away by the cloudburst of 1965.

Beyond the crossing, mire has encroached on the channel for a short way and it is supported by stone-banking. It is then crossed by the dry Cumston channel which has its own stone-banking above the foot of the hill. This leat, with a capacity unnecessarily large for domestic purposes, could certainly have provided a sufficient head of water for a mine waterwheel and I have suggested on p93 that it once fulfilled that function; it has been laboriously channelled between and beneath the hillside rocks and emerges onto a plain bounded by the eastern of the two Dry Lakes. The channel has here been driven through the centre of very old tin-works in the valley, is intersected by the Buckfast-Tavistock monastic way and the much later Wheal Emma channel and curves with the valley-side in a cutting to run between the large channel and the flowing Hamlyn's leat, taken in from O Brook just below. This upper portion of the old Cumston leat has not previously been chartered and described.

About 100yd (90m) beyond Dry Lake is a large, single-impost clapper bridge; users of the path descending the hill were enabled also to cross the Cumston leat (only 18ft below) through its having been infilled, showing that even by 1859 it was disused; the path then continued to cross Hamlyn's leat below. Two huge granite rocks impeded the channel further downstream, obstacles overcome by making bypass 'kinks' in the channel, though the lower rock still had to be cut. The O Brook valley now opens wide before the walker and the leat has attained sufficient height above it to provide a splendid view over a large expanse of the central basin backed by the prominent cone of Longaford Tor and adjacent northern heights. The valley itself, deep and strewn with medieval tin-works, is crossed at Saddle Bridge by the Hexworthy-Holne road (which passes beside Cumston Tor on the crest of Cumston Tor Hill). Beyond a small, neat clapper bridge the ancient tenement of Hexworthy appears and the leat makes an elbow bend to pass through a conduit (now infilled and surfaced) beneath the road.

The west flank of Cumston Tor provides an introduction to close-up views of the Double Dart river, here flowing from Dartmeet into its impressive gorge commencing below the tor. On rounding the spur it becomes clear that clitter impeded the leat-cutters' progress; the walker may now enjoy a view of the fine interlocking spurs in the gorge below, topped by the tors of Yar, Corndon, Vag Hill, Sharp, Mil and Benjy. The oddly shaped Cumston Tor appears above, right, and rocks and bracken on the hillside make the leat-bed the best path to follow. Dr T. A. P. Greeves presented a report in *Transactions of the Devonshire Association* 110 (1978) on Wheal Cumston Tin Mine, following his examination of the remains below and north-northeast of the tor. Greeves states that 'there is no very obvious source of water . . . for operating the water-wheel'. I would like to suggest tentatively that the old leat on the flank of Horn's Hill below the Wheal Emma was cut for that purpose, especially as Greeves gives 1849 as the latest date of documentary reference to a working mine at Cumston and field evidence shows that the leat was disused when the Wheal Emma was cut in 1859. The mine branch of the leat probably cascaded down the hill below the farm to reach its (former) launder.

A fine clapper bridge occurs as the Wheal Emma runs due south to cross the Aller Brook valley. This it does by crossing the Holne road and making its contour-loop around a large bedrock before re-crossing the road. The brook here falls into a hollow sinister both in sight and tradition – Hangman's Hollow or Pit, where a disillusioned moorman of 100 years ago, cheated into a disastrous deal at South Brent pony fair, removed his pony's halter and hanged himself rather than face his wife.

The leat, approaching the next spur (northernmost of Holne Moor) passes beneath a clapper bridge of seven imposts, beyond which the scenery becomes magnificent: Vag Hill is topped by Yar Tor, Corndon Tor rises above Easdon Combe and the fields and buildings of Rowbrook Farm; the splendid peaks of Sharp and Mil Tors have flung their clitters into the dense Miltor Wood; and flashing glimpses and sounds of Double Dart below, with Benjy Tor the sentinel pile on the south brink of the gorge, combine to make this part of the walk perhaps the most striking of any on the course of a southern Dartmoor leat. The prospect of Cumston Tor's east flank is interesting, too; it is without the line of the Cumston leat and the remaining lines are those of the Wheal Emma and Hamlyn's leats – everything in prospect without the exertion of hill-climbing!

A large clapper bridge spans the leat, which now alters course to southward; it makes an oblique crossing (now infilled) beneath the Holne road and enters the large basin containing the Venford Brook headwaters. The Venford reservoir (water supply for Paignton), its catchment area bounded by PUDC (Paignton Urban District Council) stones appears below, left, and Benjy Tor backed by the eastern highlands of the Moor beyond. Ahead is the high land of Holne Ridge and, to the right, two prominent thorn trees, where a cross-surround recently discovered by archaeologist Dr Andrew Fleming, and named by him Two Thorns Cross, forms another link in the chain of granite crosses marking the authentic 'Abbots' Way' – the monastic way between Tavistock and Buckfast abbeys – incorrectly represented on OS maps by confusing the way with the ancient 'Jobbers' Road'. The leat makes a gradual curve round the head of a T-shaped gert and reaches a clapper bridge of two openings. This entire area was enclosed and heavily farmed in medieval times; longhouses stood in the valley and a moorgate at the head of a lane passing through the farmlands; this historic lane, visible just below the leat, was the route of the monastic way between Workman's Ford on Venford Brook and Two Thorns Cross (base). The clapper bridge, erected in 1859 by the Wheal Emma leat-cutters, was obviously deemed a necessity in the light of the continuing use of the ancient way, 300 years after the monks had last followed it.

South of the Wheal Emma bridge the two leats are seen contour-looping Brockley Bottom, where are situated the main-springs of Venford Brook; the Wheal Emma was aqueducted across the valley and its high, left bank reinforced; much tin-streaming has taken place here. Beyond a clapper bridge is Ringleshutes Gert; to reach this the Wheal Emma passes a ruined longhouse and bisects the southwest corner of a medieval enclosure. A short way below the leat is seen the contour-loop of the (dry portion of) Hamlyn's leat, whilst higher in the valley is the headweir of the Holne Town Gutter. Pass another clapper and round a sharp bend in Workman's Gert, where the steep hillside is banked above the leat to prevent collapse through storm-drainage.

Now within a short distance of the Holne road and passing beneath a well-built clapper, the leat rounds the north spur of

Holne Lee, giving pleasant views over the reservoir and away to the eastern highlands. Turning due south, it bisects a reave and, once more, the monastic way to reach a double ford on the plain of the hill – 'double' because a track from the former moorgate at Sholedon fords both the (flowing) Holne Town Gutter and the (dry) Wheal Emma where the level plain facilitated the mutual (right-angle) intersection of the leats and the passage of the track. Now flowing southwest, the leat is for some way bracken-choked and shortly passes below a bridging-stone to enter the cornditch corner of a small newtake, **to which there is no public access**. Emerging from this at the east foot of Holne Ridge – with its beautiful views of the Mardle valley and the southeast border-country – the leat passes below a clapper bridge carrying the ancient Sandy Way and rounds the head of the north branch of Holy Brook. Beyond another clapper the channel then makes an elbow bend round the main source of Holy Brook and enters two enclosures (**again, no access**) at the northwest extremity of Scorriton Down, known as Scorriton Point; its final reach can be viewed, however, by approaching either from the upper Mardle valley or from Scorriton Down Gate (via Michelcombe). Walk to 681684; here the leat emerges from the Scorriton Point enclosures and passes across the corner of an old newtake; walk round the corner and observe the channel emerging from the newtake – where, if ever a bridging-stone existed none is visible below the collapsed wall – and beginning its steep drop to the Mardle valley floor. The channel-sides have been reinforced by walling, as the force of water would otherwise have caused serious erosion. William Crossing writes of remembering the cascade, which resembled that of the Devonport leat on Raddick Hill (see p21). In this case the water tumbled directly into the River Mardle, thereby bringing to an abrupt conclusion its course on the high moor.

Much of the augmented flow of the river was diverted near Brook Manor by a weir into a leat passing along the high south valley-side to a reservoir, from where water descended to a launder across the mine road (now the Manor drive) to work a large wheel. A general view of the valley, mine tips and leat channel may be seen from a gateway on the Holne-Buckfast road ½ mile (.8km) east of Hawson Cross. **There is no public access to the grounds of Brook Manor.**

11
Vitifer Leat
with branch to Wheal Caroline

6¾ miles (10.9km)   Map 6

Historical digest
The large-capacity Birch Tor & Vitifer Mine leat fell into disuse
during the years between the two world wars, but is well-
remembered as a flowing stream by many older Dartmoor
people; its channel is known to many moorland walkers as a
guide to some very fine scenery. The mine workings were on
one of the richest tin grounds of the granite mass and represent
several centuries of fruitful enterprise; there is evidence for the
working of the post-medieval mine as early as 1750. During the
1780s the Dartmoor Mining & Smelting Company was
established on the site, which is in the upper valley of the
Redwater Brook, a tributary of West Webburn. By 1796, 40
men were employed, and in 1797 a 36ft (11m) waterwheel was
installed for pumping; forty years later, when John Paull of
Tavistock was mine captain, 2 more wheels of 40ft (12m)
diameter were needed and, in 1846, 39 heads of ore-crushing
stamps were working. A period of depression followed in the
1850s, but by 1863 the mine employed 150 men. Moses
Bawden, another experienced Tavistock tin-prospector, enters
the picture in 1883; he built a small house near the Warren
House Inn which, always known as 'Bawden's Bungalow' was
demolished only twenty years ago.

A brief history of the mine, with relevant statistics, appears
in *Dartmoor Mines* by Atkinson, Burt and Waite, and in
Broughton's *The Birch Tor & Vitifer Mining Complex*. In
historical notes prepared by T. A. P. Greeves – which he has
kindly lent me – for the occasion of an organised visit to the mine,
he gives information about the final years of the mine and of the
associated working of Golden Dagger Mine downstream in the
Redwater valley. He writes:

Underground working [Vitifer] was more or less abandoned at the

96

time of the First World War, as was also the case at Golden Dagger. The last tin was removed from the dumps in 1938–39.

Also of Golden Dagger:

1931 Mine forced to close by the low price of tin (£120 per ton – cf. the present day price which at summer 1985 is £9,450).
1982 Stamps wheelpit and mine office conserved by National Park Authority.

In his article 'Dartmoor Mining Leats 1786–1836' in *Devon & Cornwall Notes & Queries* No 33, M. G. Dickinson states that 'A two mile leat was cut from the headwaters of the West Webburn above Statts Bridge on the present B3212 about the year 1793'. West Webburn does not, of course, flow anywhere near Stats Bridge, the stream in question being Stats Brook (into Walla Brook, East Dart). There is also, in my opinion, confusion over the chronology of the Vitifer and Wheal Caroline leats, it being suggested that the lengthy channel from East Dart was cut for Wheal Caroline (see p 103–4) and the Vitifer supply later 'tailed' from it. I have not found documentary or field evidence to support this statement and have therefore treated the two leats here, as the chapter heading suggests, as having the reverse chronology.

It is perhaps worth mentioning that, in the unlikely event of the Wheal Caroline leat actually having pre-dated the Vitifer, it *could* have drawn its supply entirely from North Teign country via Varracombe Brook and the North Teign river, and so not have entailed any extraction from East Dart. (Note: Dartmoor pronunciation of mine name is Vītifer, not Vītifer).

Following the leat (UP)
To follow the entire channel, including the Caroline branch, in a single-stage walk would perhaps be an undertaking not welcomed by every reader. A satisfactory and interesting way to reduce the journey is to visit the mine and the ruined miners' cottages at Cape Horn as an initial stage.

Stage 1 Take the B3212 road to Stats Bridge (668805) where a small car-park lies on the north roadside, east of the bridge. Walk eastward over the moor near the south road-side and through the outlines of 'West Cottages' which, built on the exposed shoulder of Watern Hill and known to the

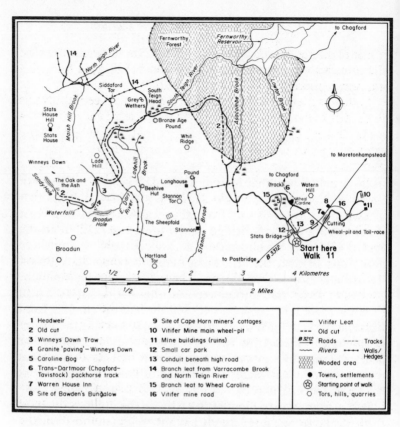

Map 6 showing Walk 11 Vitifer Leat

miners as 'Cape Horn', housed Vitifer miners and their families between 50 and 100 years ago; notice the granite steps leading to the road. Continue over the moor (below the road) until opposite the Warren House Inn; ascend to the road; walk a short way beyond the inn to a wide, stony track branching right. This is the old mine road. Descend to the valley floor and overgrown remains of the mine, including the dressing-floors and two wheel-pits (upstream from the ruined buildings). **Caution: the larger pit is dangerous; do not allow children to approach the edge**. It housed the mine's largest wheel, from which channels branched to others and the water passed down-valley to Golden Dagger Mine. The rockpile dominating the east valley-side is Birch Tor and the tremendous incisions in the hillsides, including the deep Chaw Gully, are the excavations of the miners in following the tin-lode and blasting, at first with gunpowder and, since about 1870, with dynamite.

Follow the leat uphill, where it was a torrent, keeping always to the left of a deep gert; the mine road is carried across it by a (now choked) clapper bridge of several imposts. Reaching the crest of the down (Soussons Down – pronounced 'Sow-sons') observe another deep gert nearby, the relics of Golden Dagger Mine in the valley downstream, and (eastward) the miners' path to Manaton (via Grimspound) crossing the Birch Tor-Challacombe Down col.

The leat now bends sharply to contour-loop Happy Valley, source of the East Dart tributary Walla Brook. The Warren House Inn is above, the original eighteenth-century house having stood on the south roadside with its paddock and garden enclosed when the red deer still roamed Dartmoor and provided with a cornditch. The ditch is here occupied by the leat, a distinct labour-saving move by the builders, and shortly enters a deep cutting; the scene, with bold tors, rocky gerts, the leat-cutting and the steep slope of Watern Hill above is rugged and unusual. The best walking through the cutting lies along the right bank, which is reinforced with masonry above the hillside. A large-capacity leat from the brook follows the west flank of Soussons Down to an old wheel-pit (now within the plantations), and a valley floor track leads to the ancient tenements of Walna and Runnage on Walla Brook. The intervening ground exhibits the march of progress from early medieval tin-streaming works to the capacious leats of the Victorian Industrial Revolution. More deep gerts open towards the leat, and once channelled affluents from springs and hillside drainage. A pronounced series of bends begins as the channel passes below Cape Horn; look back from here to the great gerts indenting the east Redwater valley-side between Birch Tor and Challacombe Down, the deepest of them, Chaw Gully, beside the Manaton Miners' Path.

As the leat continues to curve, the Soussons plantations recede and a fine view opens ahead of the Dart basin, with its central peak of Bellever Tor backed by the southern hill-chain. The walker, now following a northwesterly course, will soon see ahead Meripit Hill and the high road, the distant Whit

Ridge, an unpleasant marsh in the foreground known as Coal Mires, Stats Bridge and, in mid-distance, Asacombe Hill, crested by the upper boundary of the Fernworthy plantations.

The leat now passes beneath the highway through a conduit roofed by surfaced granite slabs and, on the further roadside, its grassy right bank serves as the boundary of the car park; so ends Stage 1 of the walk.

Stage 2 Again, the car park used for stage 1 is very convenient. The leat is high-banked here; follow the stony track beside the left bank. Leat and track shortly diverge, the former moving to the west side of the valley floor. Continue on the track to a point where a branch descends (left) to a ford on Stats Brook; follow this; the leat water here entered the brook from the opposite hillside and was extracted a few yards below. Cross the ford; the channel on the valley floor is choked, but its continuation is well defined as a deep, serpentine channel ascending the slope of Meripit Hill – where the water formed a cascade – and levelling out on reaching the plain of the hill; the bed has been stepped with granite on the steep to counter erosion. Notice the view across the eastern area of the central basin to Hameldon, Yar and Corndon Tors and, again, the southern hill-chain. A hut circle near the right bank retains its original, southeast-facing doorway; the extensive Caroline Bog, source of Stats Brook, appears below and on reaching the hill-crest the walker will see the West Dart tors, the dome of Wildbanks Hill, the smooth outline of Whit Ridge and the D Stone (a standing stone marked 'D' – Duchy of Cornwall – marking the Forest boundary) outside the Asacombe Hill plantations.

Next observe the branch channel (right) to Wheal Caroline (stage 3). Beyond it, right, is a small private Bronze Age 'estate' – a circular reave-wall enclosing the remains of a living hut and small ancillary building. A large mire now appears, left, under the high ridge of Meripit Hill; the leat rounds the head of the mire, is crossed by the old Fernworthy-Higher Meripit track at a crumbling cart clapper bridge of five imposts and enters Stannon Newtake, the channel being earth-blocked beneath the excellent cornditch wall. The view from the newtake is very fine, extending over the entire expanse of the central basin to the West Dart tors, the rocky hillside above the

100

Stannon Brook valley and Broadun Ring above East Dart.

Follow the leat along the upper side of the newtake as it curves towards a visible hollow under Whit Ridge; a large, flat rock affords a good seat from which to study the ever widening panorama. The central basin now lies to the left and Stannon Cottage at the foot of the newtake; the Stannon Brook valley is directly opposite with Stannon Tor above. The outline of a medieval longhouse (with a small pound to the right of it) is visible above the head-mire of the brook. On reaching the next cornditch, observe the bridging-stone for the leat which, being blocked only with loose stones, is clear to the eye.

Reaching the plain between Stannon Newtake and Whit Ridge, notice the point of a former cascade under the slope of the ridge. An older cut, which emerges from the trees (where it is now overplanted), passes beside a large, set stone over 3ft (1m) high and 3ft (1m) wide and joins the channel here; a thick growth of turf at the base of the plantation's boundary wall conceals any bridging-stone that might remain. The larger capacity main channel, meanwhile, passes beneath a fine bridging-stone in the boundary wall (near a hunting gate) and is visible beyond passing between the trees, as overplanting has not taken place in the bed of the leat – although it is blocked in places by fallen trees as it contours the north (overplanted) spur of Whit Ridge above the source-mire and valley of Asacombe (OS 'Assycombe') Brook. The Fernworthy-Meripit track is seen entering the trees on the further valley-side and the leat leaves the hill-spur to emerge into the sunlight on the north flank of Whit Ridge above the infant South Teign river. The forest-enclosed portion of the channel may be examined by walking along the forest rides.

From the high South Teign valley-side are seen Kes Tor (eastward), the celebrated Grey Wethers stone circles (right), Siddaford Tor above them and Broadun and Lade Hill (scored by the line of the leat) beyond. Notice a prehistoric pound, left, with only one stone now standing. Follow the leat across the wide plain between the head-mires of South Teign and Ladehill Brook; here, the branch leat from Varracombe Brook and North Teign descends through a twisting gully to join the main channel, and Bellever and Lough (OS 'Laughter') Tors are seen against the backdrop of the southern hills.

Several set stones appear near the leat as it passes from the plain to the flank of Lade Hill; Ladehill Bottom opens ahead and Corndon Tor, Sharp Tor and Vag Hill (Double Dart) are seen in the south. A large, trough-like, double re-entrant now appears between Lade Hill and Siddaford Tor, crossed by an old wall ascending to the tor summit. Both channels, old and more recent, are well defined as, only a few yards apart, they cross the re-entrant to follow the Lade Hill flank before rounding the spur of the hill to approach Winneys Down Traw. To see each channel, follow the higher (older) one, and on looking back to the re-entrant notice the striking 'bowl' of marshy feeders entering the stream which, in turn, once fed the leat channels.

The gradient increases on the Lade Hill spur, where boulders have been shifted by the leat-builders to make way for the channel. An entirely fresh view now opens across Ladehill Bottom: the eye can sweep from the bulky mound of Whit Ridge (left) across the small outcrops of Stannon and Hartland Tors down to the East Dart river receiving Ladehill Brook and approaching the central basin; beside the brook's left bank upstream from the confluence and just visible from this point, in a green hollow among tinners' works, is a fine beehive hut, well known to Dartmoor walkers. Beyond the river are Broadun and Higher Whiten Tor.

A wall descends from Siddaford Tor over the length of the Lade Hill spur to the river; it crosses the main leat on a bridging-stone, but none exists for the older (higher) cut, which we may assume was abandoned before this wall was built in the eighteenth century. Both channels appear clearly ahead on Winneys Down (which is incorrectly placed by the Ordnance Surveyors at Stats House Hill). At Winneys Down Traw old leat and stream intermingled, but the lower, main leat is known to have been aqueducted across the traw. The channels diverge on approaching a small rockfield, the old cut passing above it, whereas the main leat penetrates the lower portion above a ruined tor on the steep hillside below, where the sound of the rushing East Dart in the deep hole between Winneys Down and Broadun rises to the ear. The level granite platform here is weathered into pavement-like slabs, a feature unusual in granite country, and the leat, which had to be driven through it, is provided with a clapper bridge. The scene appears on the cover, the distant view extending to Hameldon, Rippen Tor and Buckland Beacon. Ahead now is the mouth of Sandy Hole, towards which the old channel is directly pointing, whilst the main leat runs from the granite 'paving' towards Waterfalls, the ruggedly beautiful fall where East Dart leaps from its upper reach peneplain to commence a transitional passage under Broadun to the middle reach in the central basin, 325ft (100m) below. The main leat passes just above this attractive scene and reaches its intake on the river at a bend. The headweir consists simply of a small boulder-wall so placed in the wide river-bed as formerly to have admitted about half of the river's flow into the channel.

The walker should now regain the upper channel and walk to its intake at 'the Oak and the Ash' – the mouth of Sandy Hole. I know no documented details of this channel, but it is not difficult to appreciate that the amount of silt washed down by the forceful river through Sandy Hole must have been disastrous for the intake, which would have become choked with every flood; indeed, the plain at the mouth of the hole is covered in sandy gravels, which also lie thickly on the river banks and account for the name 'Sandy' Hole.

As a matter of historical interest, notice the track crossing a re-entrant above the river's right bank to the left of the Oak and the Ash; it is the medieval North-South Track which traverses the entire length of the Moor to link the North and South Hams of Devon via Okehampton and Harford. The distant tor glimpsed down-valley is Rippen Tor, highest of the Hey Tor group, yet reaching the height 1,550ft (473m) only of the East Dart valley floor at Sandy Hole! Above the lonely scene rises the domed giant of the northern fen at 1,980ft (604m), Cut Hill.

Stage 3 This, like stage 1 (see p97) can easily be walked from the Stats Bridge car park and leaves stage 2 to be walked without diversion. Alternatively it can be taken in by the walker on returning from stage 2 by branching left on the plain of Meripit Hill (see p100).

Follow the branch leat; although capacious, its extraction of water from the main channel would scarcely have affected the Vitifer supply, to which it was returned by the Wheal Caroline tail-race. The leat passes across the head of Caroline Bog, where it receives an affluent, then makes directly for the northwest corner of the Caroline cornditch and passes beneath a clapper bridge; curiously, OS show only the commencing course of the leat and leave it suspended, as it were, on the edge of the mire. It is interesting that the leat-builders appear to have appropriated a part of the ancient trans-Dartmoor (Chagford-Tavistock) track as occupying the contour they needed, which plainly had dictated the position of the farm's west cornditch wall; the track descends from a junction of ways at the foot of Asacombe Hill (above, north-northwest), fords a streamlet feeding Stats Brook Head, passed originally alongside the west cornditch and ran directly to Stats Bridge. When the leat-builders arrived, they presumably diverted the old road to pass round the upper, east, cornditch, from where its junction with the original occurs at a bend below the southwest corner at 668812. This new route was eventually joined by the mine road emerging from the enclosure; a distinct hump in the road on the course of the Caroline leat suggests that a granite conduit lies below the surface. From this point follow the leat along the west flank of Watern Hill to the mine wheel-pit, situated in a deep gert near the main road. Below it, the leat tail-race passed beneath the mine road (here also the trans-Dartmoor track) and flowed into the main Vitifer Leat (see p103), so ensuring a good head of water downstream at the principal mine. The walker here rejoins stage 2.

Introduction to Canal Walks

Commercial transportation canals, including those described here, because of their function and nature are found in the British highland borderlands and lowlands rather than in the true highland zones, of which Dartmoor is one. Industrial development, housing schemes, new roadways or just sheer neglect have perhaps treated the two canals found in Part 3 of this book less harshly than many old English waterways, and it is still possible to retrace the greater part of each.

The passage of a vessel on a canal through undulating country is facilitated by lock gates; these occur always as two pairs, upper and lower, by the operation of which the channel is divided into separate compartments or 'basins'. The opening of the upper gates equalises the water level between upper channel and basin, so allowing a 'descending' vessel to enter the latter; closure of the upper and opening of the lower gates will then equalise the water level of basin and lower channel, so enabling the vessel to continue its down-country journey. In the converse case, the vessel in the basin is raised by the opening of the upper gates and can continue its up-country journey.

Three canals have been built during the last 200 years for the transporting of Dartmoor minerals. Quarried granite and mined copper ore were carried on the Tavistock Canal (opened 1817) to Morwellham for shipment on the River Tamar; this interesting channel, the work of John Taylor (see also p46) has been described by other writers. Of the two remaining channels, the history of one has been well told by M. C. Ewans in his *The Haytor Granite Tramway and Stover Canal,* but both are included in this book with detailed itinerary, to enable the reader actually to retrace the channels where still practicable. Another canal was planned in 1792 to transport mineral ores from the once flourishing mines in the Ashburton area to the navigable Dart at Totnes, but before the work was put in hand a serious slump in the minerals market occurred and the canal was never built.

12
Cann Canal

2¼ miles (3.6km)   Map 7

Historical digest

The blue slate-stone of Cann Quarry, in the lowland Plym valley, has been valued as building stone in Devon – and later much further afield – at least since 1683, when by an Indenture of 29 September of that year (25 Charles II) George Parker of 'Burringdon' (now Boringdon) in the parish of Plympton St Mary leased 'all that Holling Stone Quarry commonly called Cann Wood Quarry' to 'Nicholas Edwards the Younger of the same parish'. A century later, the grandson of the Restoration George Parker, also George, leased Cann to Thomas Manford, also of Plympton St Mary, by an Indenture of 34 George III, 1793. The 8 January 1829 saw the signing of another agreement between John, Earl of Morley – the title taken by the ennobled Parkers – and the Reverend G. A. Manley of Felton in the County of Gloucester for the lease of the quarry, 'the dwelling house called the Foreman's House, Blacksmith's Shop, Garden and Orchard belonging thereto. Also that newly erected Dwelling House, outhouse garden & orchard nearby', all for a yearly rental of £220. A decade later, George William Reeve became tenant by an Indenture of 15 February 1859 between himself and Earl John, the plan drawn to accompany the document being in part reproduced in Map ref. Conditions of rental included payment of a royalty of 6d on each ton of slate sold, and non-interference with the earl's 'salmon hutch' at the weir. Mention also appears in this document of the old canal, by then serving only as a mill leat, in which no rubbish must be tipped, as 'the mill-leat supplies with water the mill called Marsh Mills'. It is also stipulated that 'the basins situate near the canal bridge near Woodford Wood' (see p110) are in no way to be obstructed.

Cann Quarry's final phase of working life was destined to commence with the next Indenture, dated 1 April 1874, the signatories being Edmund Earl of Morley and James Gullett. (Hadfield was therefore mistaken in stating in his book that 'the

106

quarry closed in 1855'.) This final agreement specified Gullett's occupation of 'Outbuildings, yard, garden, plot called Cann House situated at Cann Quarry' and his right to 'Search for, make marketable and carry away slate', which was to be sold at the following rates:

Common Slate good quality	11s per thousand
Sawn edged & planed flooring	7d per foot.

The clause obliging the lessee to 'keep in repair' all buildings and equipment includes the terms 'machinery' and 'tramway'; although nineteen years had elapsed since the last train had run over the line, it was obviously envisaged that it might be needed again. But the South Devon & Tavistock Railway Company had opened their Plym valley line to Tavistock from the junction at Marsh Mills, and built Cann Viaduct, by 1859, and it seems probable that this newly provided means of large-capacity transport of slate from the quarry was soon adopted, a theory strengthened by two factors – the existence of a wide cart-road approaching the SD&TR (later GWR) trackside at Cann and Lord Morley's well documented, keen support for the building of the steam-traction railway.

The canal, unlike most commercial channels, does not consist of static reaches separating locks, but was constructed as a large-capacity leat with a maintained gravity flow along the lower east valley-side of the River Plym. The channel's water supply came both from the river and the Hurra or Horra Brook, a stream with a good head of water dividing Cann Wood from Hurrabrook Wood north of the quarry. A small dam 70yd (64m) up the brook's valley created a reservoir from which water was leated to the quarry planing-mill (see p113) through a launder; on leaving the mill the water of both Horra Brook and Plym leats united and passed direct to the head of the canal.

Beside an open space near the Royal Marines Establishment at Marsh Mills is a large, stone-lined basin – an intended lower terminal; it was never used, as the navigable channel remained unfinished before reaching this point (well short of the estuary), and was destined to become a white elephant. It was constructed by the Earl of Morley as a tidal wharf for the transhipment of slate from the canal to sea-going vessels. As early as 1778, John Parker – his son was created first Earl of

Morley in 1815 – had engaged John Smeaton, builder of the third Eddystone lighthouse (1759), to survey and plan for a canal from Cann Quarry to a tidal wharf, but no constructional work was begun until, at earliest, 1825, when the project was placed in the charge of the engineer J. M. Rendel. The new canal was ready in part by 1829; 'in part', because the prohibitive expense of a proposed conduit to carry it below the Plymouth-Exeter turnpike road (a plan superseded by one for a branch of the P&DR to the Coy Pool Dock) rendered its lower reach, as originally planned, superfluous. The tramroad branch was therefore extended to reach the completed dock and 'stockground' upstream in Woodford Wood. It was not long, however, before the entire canal became redundant, it being evident that constant handling and transferring of the load within such a short distance was neither speedy nor efficient, and that it would be expedient to further extend the tramroad from the dock to the quarry itself. The line, using sets both of granite and slate, was laid along the canal towpath. Correspondence between Lord Morley and the P&DR Company mentions a proposed 'junction between the new Cann Canal and the Plymouth & Dartmoor Railway . . . at Crabtree', a junction that never materialised.

The canal has no locks and was designed to take 'tug-boat' barges; after its commercial use ended (at the Woodford basin), the water continued to flow along a narrower channel to supply the waterwheel at Marsh Mills.

Following the canal (UP)

A road that formerly ran up the Plym valley on the east side of the river appears in part to have been adopted as a trackbed by the SD&TR surveyors in 1854. It started at what was called 'Fishery Gate' beside the east end of Longbridge and reached Cann Quarry on the plateau where the quarrymen's cottages were built. Its (southern) commencement coincides with Coy Pool Road.

From Marsh Mills roundabout (A38 highway, east of Plymouth) follow the Plympton sign. Cross the River Plym at Longbridge and, at traffic lights, turn left into Coy Pool Road; park on the open surfaced area (519582) between the railway level-crossing (right) and the RME (ahead). Temporary prem-

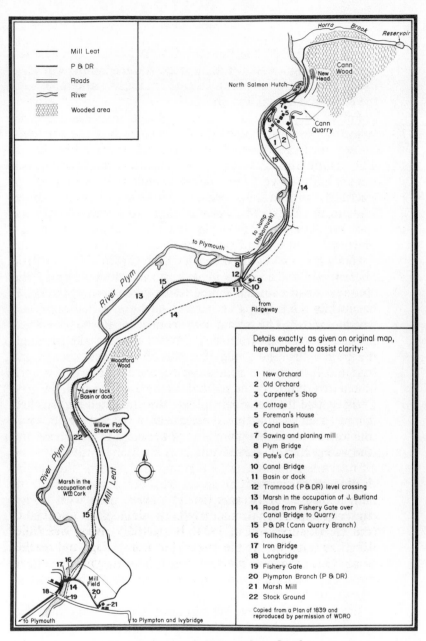

Details exactly as given on original map, here numbered to assist clarity:

1 New Orchard
2 Old Orchard
3 Carpenter's Shop
4 Cottage
5 Foreman's House
6 Canal basin
7 Sawing and planing mill
8 Plym Bridge
9 Pate's Cot
10 Canal Bridge
11 Basin or dock
12 Tramroad (P&DR) level crossing
13 Marsh in the occupation of J. Butland
14 Road from Fishery Gate over Canal Bridge to Quarry
15 P&DR (Cann Quarry Branch)
16 Tollhouse
17 Iron Bridge
18 Longbridge
19 Fishery Gate
20 Plympton Branch (P&DR)
21 Marsh Mill
22 Stock Ground

Copied from a Plan of 1839 and reproduced by permission of WDRO

Map 7 showing Walk 12 Cann Canal

ises of the Plym Valley Railway Association are seen near the right roadside as well as rolling stock and locomotives in varying stages of restoration, and a path is clearly marked between the RME and the railway above.

Follow the path (also a cycle-way), based on the Cann Quarry branch of the former P&DR of 1823; the track of the later GWR branch line from Marsh Mills to the RME has now been lifted. The rusting iron rail lying beside the path beyond the stile is a remnant of the Lee Moor Tramway, built in 1853 on the P&DR trackbed. An iron sluice occurs from which a branch channel leads to the Marsh Mills clay works, and a lower one to the riverside plain (Coy Pool) where the terminal basin is situated – presumably the channel due to be made navigable to the basin.

Half a mile (.8km) up the valley from Coy Pool is deep little Shearwood Combe. To avoid having to aqueduct the leat (ie the abortive canal) over the combe it was taken around the head, meanwhile the tramroad is carried across on a well-preserved wooden bridge. The stream in the combe appears to have dried up, and the clay pipe from the Lee Moor works is taken through the little valley and along Plymside. The plank floor of the bridge still bears the impressions of the LMT rail chairs once bolted to it. North of the combe was the 'Lower Lock, Basin or Dock' where the barge-borne slate was unloaded and stacked on the 'Stock Ground' for transfer to P&DR trucks; the dock was the lowest navigable point on the canal, from where the continuing channel served merely as the Marsh Mills leat. The channel then follows its loop round the head of the combe through an overgrown, no-access area, before passing beneath both a disused track and the GWR line, each with bridge parapets. Upstream from the 'Basin or Dock' a formidable obstacle was encountered by the canal-builders in Woodford Wood, where a rocky hill-slope rose steeply from the river's east bank. It was skilfully overcome by cutting away rock from the steep, resulting in an evenly rounded, perpendicular rock-wall rising above the canal bank.

Eventually the P&DR/LMT reaches the level of the GWR and crosses it obliquely at Lee Moor Crossing to run along the canal bank. The three lines then continue in parallel until the divergence near Plymbridge Halt of the GWR and the older lines; the former reaches the halt, whilst the latter runs to a rotting

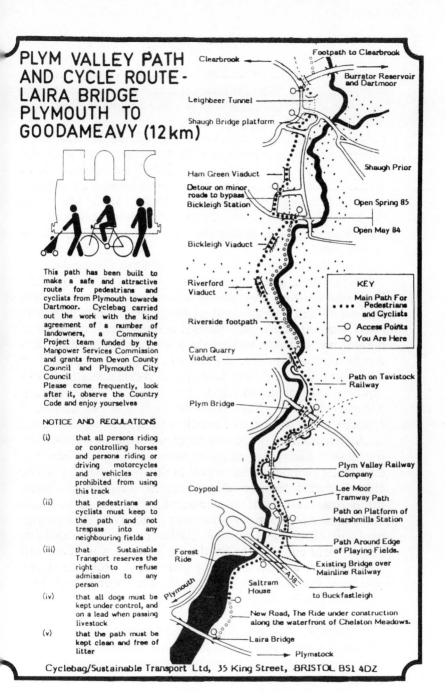

Map 8 showing Plym Valley Path and cycle route – Laira Bridge, Plymouth, to Goodameavy

wooden bridge that once carried the tramroad across the canal basin of 'Upper Dock' (near the Plymbridge road); the condition of the basin, now a swampy hollow, makes close inspection impossible. The LMT then approaches its wooden viaduct across the Plymbridge road and reaches the Cann Wood incline; the canal, meanwhile, formerly passed beneath a road bridge – 'Canal Bridge', the quarrymen called it – and the P&DR crossed at road level. Both continue together north of the road, the tramroad along the actual canal bank (Pl. 12). Two adits appear in the east bank of the canal, the first (southern) being the larger, and the smaller having a stone portal. Mining records make no mention of the adits, but it would be reasonable to assume that they were a part of Boringdon Park Mine, for which production figures for 1852–7 were: iron ore 680 tons, lead 400 tons, zinc 10 tons and silver 8,000 ounces. It is noticeable that the adits were driven without in any way interfering with the canal, but as every industrial enterprise in the area was under the ownership and scrutiny of Lord Morley, that is hardly surprising. Between adits and towpath (which follows the west bank) the bank has been cemented for a short way, and sufficient water lies in the canal bed to support a profuse spread of brilliant green burweed. The east bank then steepens and a short rock-cutting appears, beyond which the bank declines and a quarry tip comes into view – a sign that the terminus is near. The canal bed now carries a large concrete duct, and beyond the point where an old hedge, marked on the 1839 plan as 'New Orchard', comes down to the bank (below the quarry tip), there is an oblong basin, the head of the canal. From here to the quarry face a short tramroad may have been in use for transporting the stone to the basin.

Cann Quarry
Beside the basin is the ruin of the carpenter's shop – a small, square hut, its roof slates lying everywhere about. The river is very close here and a rough road, its steep bank buttressed by masonry, twists up the hillside from the canal basin to a plateau level with the head of the tip. Here are the ruins of the 'Foreman's House' and several cottages and gardens; the road meanwhile is carried over the GWR by the narrow, slatestone Cann Bridge and, passing more ruined houses, continues

eastward up the hill through Cann Wood, where it is marked on
the plan as 'Forty Foot Ride'. Near the basin was the slate-
sawing and planing mill. This once ivy-covered ruin,
resembling a small castle, is now (summer 1985) being restored
by the National Trust, owners of the property. Near the mill are
other masonry remains. The reference in an Indenture of
January 1829 to 'machinery' must mean the mill and its former
equipment; some damage was done to the Cann Quarry relics
when the Brunel viaduct of 1859 was replaced by the stone
structure of 1906–7 for the Great Western Railway. A weir in the
river, just above its crossing by the viaduct, diverted water
through a tunnel into the wheel-pit, where it powered an
undershot wheel. The pit has compartments for two
waterwheels, in one of which two axles and a gear-wheel
remained until recently; the second wheel was overshot,
supplied by the leat from the Horra Brook reservoir.

The original seventeenth-century quarry face rises from the
east bank of Plym, and a later, nineteenth-century working
known as 'New Head', was opened further from the riverside
at the foot of Cann Wood; its immense face, seen just beyond
the viaduct, rises sheer from the deep, opaque pool at its foot.

*Plate 12   Cann Canal and Cann Quarry Branch of Plymouth & Dartmoor
Railway:* Water lies in the old canal bed after heavy rain, and stone sets for the
P&DR rails are seen in the trackbed (right)

13
Stover Canal

2½ miles (4km)   Map 9

Historical digest
This short, yet fascinating waterway was the second to be built
in Devon, the Exeter Canal (1550) preceding it by over two
centuries. Engineered by Thomas Gray, Surveyor to the
Corporation of Exeter, it was constructed between 1790 and
1792 under the auspices of James Templer jnr (1748–1813) of
Stover. His father James (1722–82) had bought Stoford Lodge
estate near Newton Abbot in 1765 and built a small, dignified
mansion of Heytor granite brought down from moorland
quarries by horse-drawn wagons; in naming it 'Stover' he
preserved the local pronunciation of 'Stoford'.

Ball clay from the Bovey Basin was already in use in the
Staffordshire potteries, its carriage commencing with wagon
transport to Teignmouth Quay for shipment. James jnr
designed his canal to reach the navigable Teign from Bovey
Tracey, but funds ran out and a shorter channel had to be
constructed from a basin at Ventiford, Teigngrace. The basin
was fed by the Ventiford Brook, augmented by the Jewbridge
leat; five locks were deemed necessary and a second large feeder
from the River Teign via the Fishwick leat. Copious feeders
were essential to the canal, for L.T.C. Rolt reports in *The
Potters' Field* that 'the Royal Commission on Canals of 1906
estimated that the Stover Canal lost 26 million cu ft of water
annually through leakage and seepage'. This certainly had to be
compensated for, as by the end of the nineteenth century three
companies were using the canal, all having the bulwarks of their
barges painted in distinguishing colours: Watts, Blake &
Bearne, white; Devon & Courtenay, green; Hackney Canal
Company (see p124), black. Sailing barges were built at
Teigngrace canal basin to carry an ancient Norse rig (a square
sail on a 9ft (2.7m) mast well for'ard). A canal path was
provided for *man*-power haulage when the barges were
becalmed. As R. Russell points out in his *Lost Canals and*

Stover Canal

Waterways of Britain, the Stover Canal has a common link – clay – with 'one of the longest and busiest of the narrow Midland canals, the Trent & Mersey'. Reaching the Mersey, the clay was 'offloaded into narrow boats heading for Stoke and in particular for the Etruria Works of Josiah Wedgwood'. The Stover Canal was also used for bringing up coal, manure, limestone and sea-sand for inland use.

James jnr's fourth son George was quick to appreciate the advantages of canal transport for his granite; he constructed a crane at Ventiford Wharf, the base of which was still visible in 1960, but is now overgrown. The site of the Heytor granite tramroad on the wharfside is now a levelled field below the embankment of the BR Heathfield line, the building of which in 1865–6 for the Moretonhampstead & South Devon Railway also encroached upon it. Granite traffic on the canal ceased in 1866 when the M&SDR opened; the canal continued to carry clay, however, for a further seventy years. Watts, Blake & Bearne (WBB), always the largest clay producers in the Bovey Basin, owned a fleet of barges built at Gerry's Yard, Teigngrace. However, the challenge of competition by road transport – especially by traction-engines and the powerful Foden and Sentinel steam-wagons – after World War I, could scarcely be met by the canal. WBB had sixteen barges plying in 1931, but disposed of them in 1933, when canal traffic was rapidly declining. Their lease of the canal expired in 1942 and the then owners, British Railways Board – they had inherited the Stover Canal from the Great Western Railway who had paid £2,800 for it in 1877 – became responsible for a waterway of which the upper reach was already an overgrown, boggy ditch, a mere ghost of the canal that had carried granite for London Bridge and Bovey clay for Wedgwood's superb Staffordshire figures.

The consultative draft of a report entitled *Haytor Granite Tramroad and Stover Canal,* prepared by officers of the Devon County Council Property Department, the Dartmoor National Park Authority and Teignbridge District Council, has been sent to me for study and information; its main burden is the desirability of opening a public footpath, not only along the tramroad but along the length of the Stover Canal. It is right that readers should know of such an excellent intention, hedged about though it is at present by apparently unsurmountable

115

difficulties. Perhaps within a year or two of the publication of this book such a way for walkers may materialise.

Following the line of the canal (DOWN)
NOTE: this is best done in stages, and is so described here to assist the motoring reader to reach walking points.

Directions commence at the head basin and terminate at the canal's confluence with the navigable Teign via the Whitelake channel. Throughout its length it is closely accompanied by the former GWR Newton Abbot-Moretonhampstead branch line, now operable only to the Heathfield Industrial Estate.

Stage 1: Ventiford Wharf (848748). Park at Leygreen 150ft (137m) north of Ventiford The private house 'Ventiford' was formerly the 'Union Inn'; the last innkeeper, named Murrin, was also the blacksmith. Working where smiths of previous generations had shod the Heytor tramroad horses, Murrin gave up his occupation in 1895. The door of the inn faced the canal wharf, and tethering rings for customers' horses still remain in the wall near the doorway. Granite sets from the old tramway appear here and there in walls beside the track branching from the Teigngrace road; follow this track beneath the railway bridge; pass a wooden bridge (left) over Ventiford Brook: opposite a wooden field gate (right) stand on the brink of the stream and peer over. A weir lies in the brook where masonry sides once supported a sluice; water was here deflected into a culvert passing beneath the track into the canal-head basin, the arched culvert of the portal at the sluice can just be seen. Now enter the field gate (opposite) and walk to the actual head basin. Backed by the railway embankment and very overgrown, is the masonry of the wharf where the Heytor granite was unloaded; the rounded head of the basin is unfortunately too overgrown to reveal the feeder-conduit from Ventiford Brook. On the wharf is visible the grassy mound concealing the crane-base (see p115). The downstream end of the wharf, neatly curved, is succeeded by a culvert *beneath the canal bed* channelling land-drainage into the water-meadows beside the river; this skilful piece of water engineering has been used several times during the canal's course. The granite portal of the culvert was designed also to receive overflow from the canal. Two old iron

116

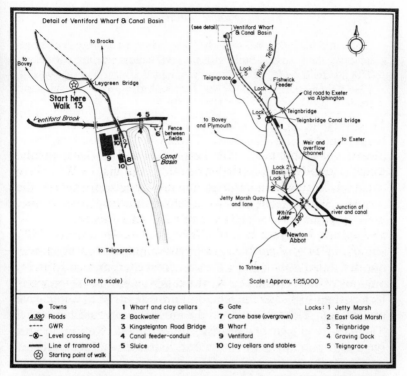

Detail of Ventiford Wharf & Canal Basin

to Brocks

to
Bovey

Leygreen Bridge

Start here
Walk 13

Ventiford Brook

4 5

Fence
between
fields

Canal
Basin

to Teigngrace

(not to scale)

(see detail)   Ventiford Wharf
& Canal Basin

Teigngrace

Lock
5

River Teign

Fishwick
Feeder

Lock
4

Old road to Exeter
via Alphington

to Bovey
and Plymouth

Lock
3

Teignbridge

Teignbridge Canal bridge

Weir and
overflow
channel

to Exeter

Lock 2
Basin
Lock
2

Jetty Marsh Quay
and lane

White-
Lake

Newton
Abbot

Junction of
river and canal

to Totnes

Scale : Approx. 1:25,000

				Locks :	
●	Towns	1	Wharf and clay cellars	6 Gate	1 Jetty Marsh
A380	Roads	2	Backwater	7 Crane base (overgrown)	2 East Gold Marsh
----	GWR	3	Kingsteignton Road Bridge	8 Wharf	3 Teignbridge
-⊗-	Level crossing	4	Canal feeder-conduit	9 Ventiford	4 Graving Dock
▬▬	Line of tramroad	5	Sluice	10 Clay cellars and stables	5 Teigngrace
✪	Starting point of walk				

Map 9 showing Walk 13 Stover Canal, with detail of Ventiford Wharf and Canal Basin

plates – they are, in fact, spaced plates with connecting bolts still in place – are set vertically in the canal bed in front of the culvert, relics of the waste-sluice that controlled the overflow.

The towpath throughout is on the east bank. On reaching a patch of impenetrable scrub (beyond a wire fence), where the canal bed holds weed-covered water, return to the head basin, noticing how aptly this was designed to give the wharf sufficient width to manoeuvre barges in the basin.

Stage 2 Drive to Teigngrace village; park near an Edward VII letter-box in a corner wall at an S-bend in the road; walk down the lane here and (with caution) over the railway level-crossing which leads to the old Teigngrace barge-building yard. Two original buildings remain, and in a broadcast in 1958 I was able to say:

One Spring evening this year I stood at Ventiford Wharf talking with Sam Gerry of Teigngrace. Sam had been a shipwright on the

117

canal, and his father before him. Here, where hens were grubbing, he'd watched barges, built with his own hands, loading with clay. The last he'd built, he told me, was named *George V* – that was in 1936. Now, barges and lock gates are rotting away in stagnant pools.

M. C. Ewans in his book gives the name of Samuel Carter, barge-builder, and The Stover Canal Co, Boat Builders, from directories of 1879 and 1906 respectively. The Gerry family took over the business shortly after World War I.

Follow the towpath northward to the downstream side of the scrub near the canal basin, so completing the link here; although there is no notice of prohibition or barred access, the walker is advised to respect the fact that **it is not a public right of way**. Return to Teigngrace boatyard and examine the canal lock 5; one balance-beam and gate have decayed, but a surprising amount of timber remains in the other gate. The Teigngrace lock basin is 110ft (33.5m) long and provides a rise in water level of 5ft 6in (1.7m). From here, the church tower and houses of Teigngrace village are nearby, downstream. Return to the boatyard, noticing how the 'water staircase' was achieved by operating the lock gates. Canal lock 4, known as the 'Graving Dock', can be approached by walking southward: again, **there is no right of way**. It was formerly possible to approach it northward from Teignbridge, but this is unfortunately no longer permissible, especially as the canal there contains water enough to nurture bulrush, common rush and several varieties of pondweed and associated wildlife, while overshadowing willows sprinkle their leaves on shining pools, a scene enriched in springtime by clumps of wild daffodils. (A huge mound east of this reach is the old Fishwick clay works).

The basin of the graving dock is 56ft (17m) long, with massive granite walls still almost perfect, and expertly curved on the left bank to form the basin. A surprising amount survives of the lock gates, one of the upper pair (now in a closed position) being almost complete. The great iron bands in which the vertical gate-beams rotated still remain. Here one can walk over the basin floor and appreciate the planning and labour that went into even a small waterway like the Stover Canal. The lower gates, wide open, are more decayed. Near the basin on the left bank is a brick-built furnace, a relic of the canal's post-War I

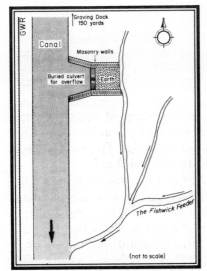

Fig 2 Granite 'bay' and feeder streams near Graving Dock

days; this was occupied, when I was last there, by a large, dead, dog fox. According to Ewans, the men who worked at the graving dock were from Teignbridge and were also responsible for lock 3. The water-level lift effected at lock 4 was the greatest on the canal – 6ft 9in (2m). Below the dock will be seen a granite bay opening onto the parallel drainage ditch; in addition to serving as an overflow channel this may have provided a mooring for small boats used by canal maintenance men (Fig 2).

Stage 3 Before leaving Teigngrace, the walker should visit the church, with which so many members of the Templer family have been associated. (The key is obtainable from Mrs E. A. Buttigieg of 1, School Road, parallel with the church entrance-drive.) Teigngrace Church is a pleasing little building in Georgian Gothic, known to architects as 'Strawberry Hill Gothic', with characteristic wooden windows painted battleship grey and having clear glass. A plaque on the west face of the tower reads:

> Church erected in the Year of Our Lord 1787 by James Templer Esq and the Revd John Templer Rector of Teigngrace.

The building, dedicated to St Peter and St Paul, is probably the fourth to occupy the site. The earliest, of timber, was succeeded by one of stone which was demolished in the fifteenth century to make way for another building licensed by Bishop Stafford of

119

Exeter (Stafford Episcopal Register). Neglect during the eighteenth century caused this third church to fall into progressive decay, until the enterprising Templers restored a sense of the dignity of village worship by erecting the present substantial building. The large altar-piece is a copy by James Barry, BA, of Van Dyck's painting 'Pieta' (Peter) in the Antwerp Museum. The deaths of several Templers are commemorated on wall-tablets, including James the canal builder (1813), George the granite tramroad builder (1843), and the rector, the Reverend John(1832). Later Templers were James (1882), Arthur Henry (1930) and, outside in the peaceful well-kept churchyard, Commander James Templer RN was buried in 1979.

Cottages of cob and thatch and old farmhouses are scattered about the village, one unusual in Devon in having no pub! The marshes in the vale, where bulrushes and water plants burgeon picturesquely, are alive with the sounds of waterfowl and smaller marsh birds and extend beyond the canal and the River Teign almost to the foot of the Haldon Hills. This easterly barrier makes a declining sweep towards the coast, forming a backdrop to a delightful piece of rural England inevitably destined to be ravished by the march of 'progress' in the form of the Teignbridge clay giant.

Stage 4 Drive southward and turn left at the T-junction into the Teignbridge road. Cross the long bridge over the marshes, the railway level-crossing and the canal bridge. Turn immediately right into a yard beside a row of old buildings and ask permission of Mr Sam Payne to park. If he is not at the yard, he is still willing for readers to park – a concession, near this busy narrow road, much to be appreciated. The extent of the canal's decay and encroaching development near Teignbridge makes it impossible to see what M. C. Ewans saw only two decades ago. The two bridges carrying the road here are known as 'Teignbridge' and 'Teignbridge Canal Bridge'. When the former was rebuilt in 1815, evidence was found of three previous structures, indicating the importance of this crossing-place since medieval times; they were, respectively, of wood, red sandstone, and slate-stone. On the right bank is a lorry-breaker's yard; ask permission to enter to view the canal bank, where only a few gate-timbers of lock 3 now remain. Notice a plaque and emblem on the north parapet of the canal bridge; the emblem, a ram's head, is thought to signify the ancient ram-roasting feast at Kingsteignton, which was celebrated on Whit Monday; the feast lapsed for some years after 1962 but has since been reinstated. Ram sandwiches are in great demand at the feast, when a May Queen is crowned and a gymkhana held. At the 1961 Feast (23 May), 1,800 people paid for admission and a ton of logs was consumed in roasting a 140lb (63.5kg) ram on a spit for 5 hours. The wording of the plaque is unreadable from the canal banks and I am indebted to Mr H. W. Castleton of the breaker's firm for his assistance in climbing a ladder from the canal bed: the wording is:

> Erected by order
> Thomas Taylor Esq
> Revd Thomas Kirson
> Revd W. B. Wrey
> Magistrates of this County 1798.

Cross the main road; the long line of old buildings, many granite-buttressed on each side, are clay cellars. The east side (furthest from the canal) is now Mr Sam Payne's yard, and beyond a gate at the lower end are the premises of Messrs A. Neild, commercial vehicle dealers. In order to see the canal side of the clay cellars and the continuing waterway, telephone Mr Payne on 0626-2942 before setting out; to pass through the lower yard request the permission of Mr A. Neild or his foreman. A large metal security gate is swung across the yard when staff are not present, so **do not attempt to pass beyond it**.

From the far end of the lower yard can be seen the large, elongated clay-tip (of WBB) reaching to the very bank of the canal, constituting an area of no access.

Stage 5 Drive into Newton Abbot, following Exeter signs. Shortly before Kingsteignton Road Bridge are traffic lights (and a BR sign pointing to the right); here turn abruptly left into Jetty Marsh Lane and continue to where two old buildings stand; one (the smaller) was a stable and the other a clay cellar – it later housed a cider-press – used many decades ago by the former Devon & Courtenay Clay Company, which was absorbed in 1962 by WBB. Park at the junction of lanes. Follow the green lane past the clay cellar to the abutments of a bridge (span removed) across the Whitlake channel (see below). Beside the bridge is a small creek facing the clay cellar; on the further bank is something now rare, and unfortunately in an advanced state of decay – the ribs and keel-board of a Stover Canal barge, the ribs encased in mud and concealed by weeds. Beyond the bridge is the site of the old pits and adits of Devon & Courtenay's West Gold Marshes workings, this firm having also despatched clay by canal barge from Jetty Marsh Quay (next to be described). The workings were infilled many years ago by the simple expedient of dumping ash from the furnaces of Newton Abbot's former large, coal-fired power station. The Whitelake channel here was used for floating clay barges from West Gold Marshes to the navigable Teign.

To explore the Jetty Marsh Quay and the canal basin it is necessary to visit each canal bank. Drive or walk to the office of Messrs Bryan Cowell Builders Ltd (left, a short way along the lane) just before reaching the tanks of F. J. Emery Oils Ltd. The inquiry office is inside the gate, left; call and ask permission to see the old building at the canal side; this has an undulating roof-ridge and, built within recent years, a frontal annexe bearing a signboard with the firm's name. The original building was the coal and clay cellars of Jetty Marsh Quay. Ahead, left, is the canal basin and masonry of locks 1 and 2; sharp left is the Whitelake channel, a leat cut in the early nineteenth century to drain Jetty Marsh and, centre, a backwater. The continuing Whitelake channel, suitably deepened and widened, forms the final reach of the Stover Canal, and alongside it is Jetty Marsh Quay. Beyond the fence, left, is the yard of R. C. Motors; here, now regrettably destroyed, were a slipway and hand-operated cable-drum for hauling up barges in need of repairs; on the west side of Jetty Marsh opposite the slipway, its ruins now hidden among undergrowth and trees, was the cottage of the Jetty Marsh lock-keeper, the last being Fred Lang, one of whose brothers was drowned in the canal basin.

I am indebted for information about this locality to Mr Sydney King of Newton Abbot, who actually rented the clay/coal cellars on the quay before World War II, when the few remaining barges were being beached – one of them, the relic beside the creek mentioned above. Sydney remembers the waterway in constant use, with large barges bringing coal from coasters to the quay, and he customarily drew up his own boat on the slipway now displaced by the R. C. Motors' yard. Again looking across the water, notice a wooden footbridge spanning another creek and, some distance to the right, the arches of Kingsteignton Road Bridge. Parking space in Jetty Marsh Lane is very restricted and before approaching the further, east bank of the canal it is wise to leave a car at the junction near the lane-end and go on foot. Walk to the main Kingsteignton road; turn left, cross the Whitelake (west end of road bridge) and enter a gateway, left; follow a public footpath between canal and BR line. It leads directly to the footbridge mentioned, the creek on the east bank being an overflow channel from lock 2 on the canal (see below). Cross the footbridge; the path leads to the site of the canal basin, 215ft (65.5m) long, 45ft (13.7m) wide, where four iron mooring bollards are seen and barges were moored to await the rising tide. The remains of locks 1 and 2 are visible, the masonry walls being perfect but the gates fast decaying. The balance-beams of two gates have been pulled into the copse beside the basin, where they lie rotting. Above the head of the basin is the BR bridge over the canal and, beyond it, lock 2, where a sluice controlled the escape of water into the overflow channel and the canal curved to round the east verge of Jetty Marsh to reach the Whitelake channel. It is not possible to inspect lock 2 without crossing the railway line; to do so **can be dangerous and involves trespass on BR property**.

Return to Kingsteignton Road Bridge; cross to the east parapet and view the final reach of the canal. A high concrete platform is seen above the right bank where the canal makes a slight easterly bend; this marks the final reach, which cannot be approached on land without first obtaining permission at the SWEB Testing Station in Wharf Road: ask for Mr K. A. Ballamy, senior foreman, and show a copy of this book. Features to be seen are some remaining masonry of the old wharf (from which the approach road is named), the metal base of a crane in which the vertical iron post rotated, and the end of the canal. To the wharf, barges and coasters once brought coal for the former steam-powered generating station (since demolished). Above it runs the concrete platform seen from Kingsteignton Road Bridge; this is the relic of a later method (abandoned when the power station was demolished) of delivering coal, for here, at railway sidings constructed for the purpose, coal was discharged from rail trucks onto a conveyor belt which carried it to the furnaces. The sidings were elevated to facilitate the movement of coal trains branching from the main line at bridge level. With the necessary permission, therefore, walk the length of the concrete platform and descend from it to the canal bank below the railway bridge. Follow the canal for its remaining few yards and stand at the confluence of Whitelake and Teign – the end of the Stover Canal. At the time of writing, SWEB have plans to sell this part of their property; the effect on access, which is unlikely to materialise for a considerable time, will have to be judged by the walker on the occasion of his visit. L. T. C. Rolt writes in *The Potters' Field*:

All clay traffic on the canal had ceased by 1938. The first overseas shipments from Teignmouth appear to have gone to Ireland, Calais and Quebec, but by 1863 Genoa, Seville, Bordeaux, St Malo and Dordrecht had been added to the list of destinations for ball clay. A decade later the European market had widened still further to include Riga, Egersund, Stockholm, Brussels, Antwerp, Lisbon, Leghorn and Rouen . . . All this overseas clay traffic started its long journey by being loaded into barges on wharves on the Hackney and Stover canals (the former being a short supplementary canal from a tidal backwater in Kingsteignton parish to the estuary and Teignmouth).

As I stood at the confluence of the Stover Canal and River Teign on a cold March day a large cob swan, feathers ruffled by a fierce wind, sailed from river into canal and passed before me towards the old coal wharf. His was a markedly silent passage; in audible contrast on either side were the sounds of articulated lorries crossing Kingsteignton Road Bridge and a '125' on the main railway line from Exeter entering Newton Abbot station. It was surely an appropriate place to stand and reflect on the dramatic changes in means of transportation since the granite and clay barges sailed past into the navigable Teign, making for New Quay at Teignmouth for the despatch of their loads to many and distant destinations.

Bibliography

Anonymous. *The Village of Horrabridge on the Edge of Dartmoor* (printed by Penwell, Callington, 1975)

Atkinson, M., Burt, R. and Waite, P. *Dartmoor Mines* (Department of Economic History, University of Exeter, 1978)

Baring-Gould, Sabine. *Sheepstor* (Hoyten & Cole, Plymouth, 1912)

Booker, Frank. *Industrial Archaeology of the Tamar Valley* (David & Charles, 1967)

Broughton, D. G. *The Birch Tor and Vitifer Mining Complex* (*Transactions Cornish Inst of Engineers*, 1968/9)

Dickinson, M. G. 'Dartmoor Mining Leats 1786–1836', *Devon & Cornwall Notes & Queries, No 33* (1974–7)

Ewans, M. C. *The Haytor Granite Tramway and Stover Canal* (David & Charles, 1977)

Hadfield, Charles. *Canals of South West England*, vol 3 of Canals of the British Isles (David & Charles, 1967 and 1985)

Harris, Helen. *Industrial Archaeology of Dartmoor* (David & Charles, 1972)

Hemery, Eric. *Historic Dart* (David & Charles, 1982)

———— *High Dartmoor: Land and People* (Robert Hale, 1983)

———— *Walking the Dartmoor Railroads* (David & Charles, 1983)

Howarth, Frank. *The Plymouth Water Undertaking*, paper prepared for the Institute of Municipal and County Engineers (1934)

Morley Estate Papers, in West Devon Record Office, Plymouth

Review and Report on Mills supplied by the Plymouth Leat (Plymouth City Council, 1854)

Robins, John. *Follow the Leat*, 2nd edition (John Robins, Tavistock, 1984)

Rolt, L. T. C. *The Potters' Field* (David & Charles, 1974)

Russell, R. *Lost Canals and Waterways of Britain* (David & Charles, 1982)

Transactions of the Devonshire Association

Dines, H. G. *The Metalliferous Mining Region of South-west England* Vol II (HMSO 1956)

Bray, Mrs A. E. *A Description of the Part of Devonshire bordering on the Tamar and the Tavy* (John Murray, London, 1836)

Index